While every precaution has been taken in the preparation of this book, the publisher assumes no responsibility for errors or omissions, or for damages resulting from the use of the information contained herein.

MYSTERIOUS MURDERS: TRUE CRIME TALES OF UNSOLVED MURDER CASES AND MYSTERIOUS DEATHS

First edition. May 20, 2022.

Copyright © 2022 Drew Creeden.

ISBN: 979-8201446048

Written by Drew Creeden.

Table of Contents

Mysterious Murders: True Crime Tales of Unsolved Murder Cases and Mysterious Deaths

By Drew Creeden

Quick note for the reader: this book is written in British English.

Dedicated to victims of crimes still seeking justice.

Introduction

I remember when I was a child and my parents switched on a JonBenet Ramsey documentary one evening. It must have been a weekend since I was allowed to stay up late and watch the show with them, and I recall this documentary being the first true crime show I really engaged with. Crime shows on an evening were a common occurrence in my household, be it true or fictionalised, but usually they were just on in the background while I played with my toys or entertained myself. However, for whatever reason, this particular show caught my attention. Perhaps it had something to do with JonBenet being a similar age to me at the time, so when I saw her face on the screen, I kept watching. I took myself to the floor in front of the TV and watched from beginning to end.

Unlike most films, cartoons and TV shows I'd seen up until that point, there was no conclusion to this story. The bad guy wasn't caught. There was no justice for the victim. I was devastated.

My young brain couldn't verbalise how I felt, but I was heartbroken. I couldn't (and still can't) comprehend why someone would do this. I was concerned that someone had killed an innocent child and nobody was going to jail for it. My young mind was racing, and I wanted to find the answers. I would ask my parents why this happened, and they would tell me that although there were bad people in the world that it wouldn't happen to me because they would protect me. This offered little comfort to me - I wanted to know who killed the little girl and why. I would watch the news every night after watching the documentary, hoping to see the murderer appear on the news in handcuffs as he was being led to jail. Sadly, as we now know, that scenario is unlikely to ever happen.

Still, the fascination with unsolved crimes and mysteries remained with me as I grew up. It seems like mysterious murders also affected a lot of other people, too, as we can see in the surge of true crime podcasts dedicated to solving crimes that have gone unpunished. While justice is the ultimate outcome for any crime, I still think it's important to remember the victims of unsolved crimes and to make sure their stories don't get forgotten.

With that in mind, I set out delving into murders and suspicious deaths from recent history. To put yourself in the shoes of the victim's family is an impossible feat and an unbearable thought. The notion that your loved one was brutally slaughtered and the killer or killers get to live their life as normal is too much for many of us to comprehend. The cases in this book don't have the closure of a killer brought to justice, which makes their tales important ones to remember.

There are eleven cases in this book, each posing their own questions and unexplained acts of violence. While each case is different, they all have one unanswered question in common:

Who carried out this horrific murder?

What Happened to Tara Calico?

The mysterious disappearance of a teen girl who vanished after going on a bike ride was headline news when a Polaroid picture was found, allegedly of her, showing her gagged and bound.

Tara Calico was getting ready to go for a bike ride on the morning of September 20, 1988. The sun had risen, and it was looking like it was going to be a pleasant day, of which there were many in the New Mexico city of Belen, where Tara lived with her mother and stepfather. The 19-year-old started this day out like she did most days. She got up, had breakfast, got ready and set out on a 36-mile ride on her trusty mountain bike. Tara enjoyed these outings, and her mother, Patty Doel, used to accompany her daughter on these rides until she noticed a motorist was stalking her as she rode. Patty soon decided the route wasn't safe and stopped going out on her bike, urging her daughter to do the same. However, Tara wouldn't let strange men ruin her hobby and committed to going out every morning without her mother by her side.

On this particular morning, before embarking on her regular jaunt up to New Mexico State Road 47, Tara asked her mother for a favour: if she wasn't back by midday, she would need to be picked up because she had plans that afternoon. The mother readily agreed to collect her if she saw no sign of her by noon, and Tara took off on her ride.

Before she knew it, Patty looked at the time and saw it was nearing midday. With Tara still out, she got in her car and went to pick up her daughter. She drove up and down the highway that Tara always rode on. Concerned that she couldn't see Tara, she drove up and down the route again with still no sign of the young girl. Panic set in for Patty, who quickly called the Sheriff's Department in Valencia County to report Tara as missing. Police arrived and scoured the area, with state police being called in to assist. The local community also stepped up, and hundreds of locals combed the area for clues as to what happened to Tara. Some pieces of evidence were uncovered, and they weren't promising. First was Tara's Walkman, which she always had when she went out on a ride. The second was a set of bike tracks that looked like they'd skidded, suggesting a quick getaway or a struggle between the driver and Tara.

Nobody saw the teen being taken or attacked, but a handful of people all reported the same thing: Tara was riding in the direction of her home at around 11:45 am. The same witnesses who reported this also told police about an old pickup truck tailing the teen as she pedalled home. Each of them noted something distinctive about the truck, too: it was carrying a shell camper. Aside from these witness observations, the police had nothing else to go on. It seemed like the case was so cold so quickly that it was a lost cause. Until, the following year, when a macabre discovery was made.

The Infamous Polaroid Pictures

A woman was coming out of a convenience store in Florida, and as she headed back to her vehicle, she noticed something that caught her eye on the parking lot floor. She picked it up and was disturbed by her find. It was a polaroid image of a young woman, bound at the wrists and legs with duct tape wrapped around her mouth. The terrified girl in the picture wasn't alone, either. There was also a little boy in the twisted photo, bound and gagged. The woman raced to call the police and hand over what could be crucial evidence of an unsolved kidnapping. All she knew was that just before she picked the polaroid up, a Toyota van had been parked in that space, and she assumed the photo had fallen out without the owner knowing. The driver was a man, possibly in his thirties, although this was hard to tell because he had a thick moustache that covered the lower half of his face. It was a race against time for police to find this man, and they set up roadblocks around Port St. Joe to capture the suspect. It seems they were too late, as the van was never found. Further inspection of the image revealed that the photo was taken after May 1989 due to the type of film it used.

A Current Affair, a news programme, aired the disturbing image on their show a month after it was discovered. Patty Doel and her husband hadn't seen the show but found themselves with an influx of calls from friends who had seen it. They all told the Doels the same thing: the girl in the image was the double of Tara. The young boy in the image was recognised too, with the family of missing Michael Henley receiving a similar spate of calls from family members who watched the show. The two sets of families worked with the police to work out if the youngsters in the picture were indeed their missing children. After thoroughly reviewing the polaroid, both Patty and Michael's mother attested that it was their children in the photo. Patty noted that Tara had unique scarring on her right thigh, as did the young woman in the picture. She was beyond sure this was her little girl. To add to her certainty, the kidnapper had placed a copy of the book *My Sweet Audrina* next to Tara. It was her favourite book.

Still, a second and third opinion was sought out. Scotland Yard analysed the picture and confirmed it was Tara. Los Alamos National Laboratory also received the photo but concluded that it *wasn't* Tara in the picture. To try and ascertain the validity of the possible evidence, it was also sent to the FBI, who couldn't decide if the girl in the picture was Tara.

The following year, Michael Henley's parents received the news they'd been dreading since his disappearance. His decomposing body was found in a mountain range close to the place he was last seen in 1988. This ruled out the possibility of it being Michael in the polaroid next to Tara. Nobody was ever apprehended for the death of the young boy, and it was decided that murder was unlikely. A more likely scenario was that the nine-year-old took off and got lost, eventually succumbing to hypothermia.

The Tara Calico case has blown hot and cold over the decades. In 2008, a renewed interest in the case arose when Rene Rivera went public with his thoughts. The sheriff claimed that two young men had been driving behind Tara's bike and struck her with their vehicle. In a panic, Rivera stated the boys bundled Tara into their truck and killed her. He went on to say that other people knew of the crime and were complicit in the coverup. It was even suggested that the culprit's parents may have been the ones to aid the young men in disposing of all evidence.

In 2009, the Port St. Joe police department was sent a photo of a little boy with his mouth drawn over in a black pen, as if mimicking black tape, presumably trying to imitate the 1989 image of the unidentified boy previously thought to be Michael Henley. The police chief was subsequently sent another photo of the same boy, this time untampered. Around the same time, *The Star* was sent the same image, and the newspaper immediately sent the photo to the police. The same day they did this, another peculiar occurrence happened at the Gulf County Sheriff's Department.

A woman had called in, claiming to be a psychic. She told the police that she knew where Tara was buried and that she'd worked with her in a strip club prior to her murder. She even gave a location in California as to where Tara's remains were, but police searches revealed nothing. Ultimately this call was dismissed as fake, but it's worth noting the uncanny timing.

Years passed, and it seemed the case was as cold as it was ever going to get with no leads in sight. Still, a 2013 deathbed confession would cause the case to be reopened. Henry Brown knew his time on earth was almost up, and there was one thing he needed to get off his chest before he departed our world: he knew who killed Tara.

Police attended Henry's bedside and listened as he told them exactly who killed Tara and the events that led to her murder.

The Deathbed Confession

Henry was in the basement of Lawrence Romero Jr when he made a shocking discovery. A young girl's body crudely wrapped in sheeting lay on the cold basement floor. When Henry asked Lawrence about the corpse, he was told the full story.

Lawrence and his buddies, Dave and Leroy, drove behind Tara as she rode her bike that fateful morning. They were working on getting the young woman's attention and, in doing so, ended up accidentally running her over. They had no intention of helping her - they took her to a desolate area and raped her. Tara was still alive at this point, and the group of men decided to haul her into the truck and drive off with her.

Tara told her attackers that she would go to the police, prompting the trio to decide stabbing her to death was the best option. The two men restrained Tara as Lawrence used the knife to stab her multiple times. Lawrence's dad was Sheriff at the time, and he told Henry this is why he was able to get away with it. Henry went on to say that Lawrence Jr had penned a note to confess his crimes, but Lawrence Sr had destroyed it. Henry's confession didn't lead to any arrests. Lawrence Jr died in 1990 in an apparent suicide, although his father maintains he was murdered.

In 2019, the FBI announced a $20,000 reward for any information that led to justice for Tara.

Patty Doel passed away in 2006, but her hope of reuniting with Tara never dimmed. She kept the faith that her daughter was alive, perhaps as a way to deal with her traumatic disappearance as well as give her something to keep on living for. The polaroid, as disturbing as it was, offered Patty the idea that her daughter was still out there, which offered the mother some kind of comfort that they'd be together again someday. Patty's husband, John, and her son Chris didn't share the same glimmer of hope. They both believe that Tara is gone forever and that her ever turning up alive is highly unlikely. It seems like they might be right, but we can't ever dismiss the hope of finding out the truth.

The Villisca Axe Murders

The gruesome Villisca Axe Murders occurred in Iowa in the summer of 1912. Despite there being numerous suspects, two trials, and even a confession, authorities are still stumped to this day as to who committed the bloody massacre.

The small town of Villisca, Iowa, has a population of just over 1,100 and offers a true sleepy, tight-knit town feel. There are a number of churches huddled together not far from the local middle school, which is situated close to the picturesque Hacklebarney Woods. The neighbourhood is filled with white houses, home to families who have lived in the town for generations. One of those houses, however, is different to the rest. Its presence is ominous and sinister. There are no lights on in this house when the sun sets, and no family inside settling down for the evening. There are never any children playing on the lawn, and its exterior looks unkempt compared to its surrounding houses. A sign has been placed in front of the porch, written in red, scrawled, blood-like writing: *The Villisca Ax Murder House*.

Still, this now-desolate house was once a home bustling with life. Josiah Moore and his wife Sarah brought their four children up in the property, which was as affluent as they were. Their children consisted of three boys and a girl; Herman was their firstborn, followed by Mary, then Arthur and baby Paul. The Moores were well-known and well-liked in the small but close community, and on June 9, 1912, they were partaking in some community activities with their church. Sarah was coordinating the Children's Day Programme, to which she brought all of the family. She'd also allowed Mary to invite her two friends, eight-year-old Ina Mae and 12-year-old Lena Gertrude Stiållinger, to stay at their house after the family activities had ended. The family, plus the two girls sleeping over, got home around 10 pm that night. They would only survive for a few more hours after settling in for the night - little did they know, someone was in the attic, waiting patiently until they could crawl out of the shadows and brutally slaughter the family.

When the intruder felt it was safe to come out of his hiding place, he did so with an axe in hand. He spotted an oil lamp and set it off to burn low enough to guide his way through the darkened property, but not so bright that people would wake up. Then, quietly, the trespasser made their way to the master bedroom and lifted the axe over their head before raining blow upon blow on Josiah's face. The sharp blade had mutilated the father-of-four's face so badly that his eyes were no longer intact by the time the attacker ceased battering his face. Then, the killer turned their weapon around and used the blunt end of the axe to beat Sarah to death. After eliminating the bigger threats - the only adults in the house - the attacker headed over to the children's rooms and again used the blunt end of the weapon to bludgeon the youngsters one by one.

The eldest child in the home, Lena, appeared to have tried to fight back. While Sarah and her children may have been asleep when the attacker pummelled them - therefore incapacitated before they could have any chance of escaping - Lena was seemingly awake. The killer likely woke her up after murdering the other children, as he went back to Moore's marital bed to attack them a second time with the axe, despite the fact they were likely to have already been dead by this point. He then went downstairs where Lena and Ina were, fatally attacking the younger girl before setting his sights on the elder, who used her arms to try and defend herself. The killer landed harsh blow after harsh blow onto Lena's head and upper body before she succumbed to her injuries. As she lay lifeless on the bed, it's speculated the intruder sexually assaulted the 12-year-old. She was naked from the waist down, and her nightdress had been pushed up, suggesting she had been molested.

When he was done slaughtering the Moore family and their guests in the early hours, the killer picked up the house keys and left, locking the door before departing.

With Villisca being so close-knit, the neighbours naturally all look out for one another. They were familiar with each other's routines and habits, so when the Moores still hadn't emerged from their property by 7 am to complete their morning chores, members of the community became concerned. Mary Peckham, who lived next door, had been looking out of her window for some time, expecting the Moores to come out and tend to their chickens as they normally would have done by this time. Growing increasingly worried that something was up, she walked over and knocked on their door. She waited a minute or so and knocked again when nobody answered. She went to open the door but found that it had been locked. She headed to their garden for further inspection and let Moore's chickens out before airing her worries to Josiah's brother. Ross Moore headed over to his siblings' property and knocked, yelled, and banged before coming to the disturbing realisation that nobody was going to answer the door.

Ross fetched his copy of the key to the house and went in to see what the situation was while Mary stood on the porch. Ross made his way to the guest bedroom, where he was greeted with a horrific sight: Lena and Ina, covered in their own blood, lying lifeless on the bed. He ran out to Mary, telling her she needed to call the peace officer, Henry Horton. She raced home to do so while Ross waited at the gory scene.

Henry raced over as soon as he received the panicked call from Mary and proceeded to search the property. He would discover everyone in the Moore household had been brutally slain, and he also uncovered the weapon - the axe that belonged to Josiah. Oddly, they also found a slab of bacon had been taken from the fridge and left in the living room. Perhaps the attacker was planning on stealing the food or was going to make himself a snack but decided not to; regardless, it was an odd find at the murder scene. There was also a bloodied bowl of cold water discovered, and police surmised that the murderer had used this to clean his hands.

Soon, the property was filled with members of the community: doctors, the police, a coroner, and a minister had all been summoned to the murder house, and with it being such a small community, the townspeople of Villisca were all quick to hear about the horrific events. The horror story spread like wildfire, and pretty soon, hundreds of the townsfolk were gathered outside of the crime scene. One of the residents also took part of Josiah's broken skull as some kind of memento of him.

After the shock had somewhat simmered, the people of Villisca now wanted to find the perpetrator of the sick crime. However, police had little to no leads on the case and found themselves haphazardly searching the nearby woods in the hope of uncovering some evidence. Bloodhounds found no clues, there were no witnesses, and any semblance of the crime scene had long gone since the house was now an attraction for the local folk.

The Suspect List

Suspect #1: Reverend George Kelly

Kelly was a travelling minister who was visiting Villisca to attend the Children's Day services that Sarah had helped put together. He was, by all accounts, viewed as a strange man. He'd suffered a mental breakdown as a young man, and as he developed into adulthood, he was accused a number of times of harassing women. He was known as somewhat of a peeping Tom and had approached several young girls and tried to proposition them, asking them to strip off and pose for him. The day before the Villisca Axe Murders, he came to town and partook in the Children's Day activities. He then left the following day in the early hours of the morning, on or shortly after 5 am.

After his departure from Villisca, Kelly developed an obsession with the axe massacre. He penned letters to not only the police investigating the case but also to relatives of the victims. Strange behaviour indeed, even for a man known to be peculiar and show delinquent tendencies (particularly towards women). A private investigator wrote back to Kelly, flattering him while probing for some information about the murders, to which the reverend replied with an abundance of information about the case. He spoke of hearing noises coming from the house while out walking. He told of hearing the thud of the axe being struck and explained how he saw the killer disturbed by passersby and had stood on the porch until they'd left eyeshot. However, Kelly was known to suffer from mental illnesses, which caused police to discredit his version of events. Plus, his role as a minister made authorities think a person in such a position wouldn't carry out such a savage murder. After a while, Kelly slipped away from the police radar until 1914, two years after the massacre occurred.

Kelly found himself in trouble with authorities after sexually harassing a young woman who had previously applied for an advertised job working for him. When he was arrested for sending the woman obscene letters, he was shipped off to a mental institute and found himself yet again on the suspect list for the Villisca Axe Murders. Three years later, he was eventually arrested for the Moore family massacre. Much to everyone's surprise, Kelly made a full confession to the crimes, although perhaps not in the most ideal of circumstances; he did so after hours upon hours of police interrogation. As we now know, police practises back in the early 1900s weren't against using brute force to encourage a confession. As such, Kelly recanted his admission of guilt, but his trial for murder still went ahead.

The case against Kelly had four main components: first was his disturbed mental state and his obsession with sex. Secondly, police were made aware of a blood-stained shirt he sent off to be cleaned just a week after the killing took place. Thirdly, Kelly displayed a thorough knowledge of the murder, and lastly, he had previously made a full confession. The charges against him focused specifically on the murder of Lena Stillinger. The sexual pose she was left in tied in with Kelly's preference for asking women to pose naked for him. The young girl had been pulled slightly off the edge of the bed, where a lamp was placed underneath her at the foot of the bed. The state insisted that Kelly had done this for visual sexual gratification.

The court was made aware that Kelly had been caught peeking in women's bedrooms just days before the killing and was known to roam the streets at all hours. They were also offered evidence of Kelly begging two 13-year-olds to pose naked for him.

However, Kelly was eventually acquitted of the murders, leaving the victims' remaining family and the town of Villisca at a loss as to who among them had committed such an atrocity.

Suspect #2: Frank Jones

Villisca resident Frank Jones was also an Iowa State Senator. Josiah previously worked for Frank at the implement store he owned, spending a number of years there as an employee before he handed in his notice to open his own shop. This move reportedly took a lot of business away from Frank's store, which reportedly included a lucrative John Deere dealership. On top of this, Josiah Moore was speculated to have been engaging in a sexual affair with Frank's daughter-in-law. However, this is just a rumour, and there is no solid evidence to support this.

Hearsay also suggests that Senator Frank Jones hired William Mansfield, a prime suspect in similar unsolved murders, to slaughter the Moores. This is still just another unproven allegation, however.

Suspect #3: Henry Lee Moore

Henry Lee Moore, no relation to the slain Moore family, was a killer who murdered his mother and grandmother shortly after the Villisca axe massacre. His preferred weapon when slaying his family was an axe. In the lead up to the double-murder, Moore had been writing to a 16-year-old girl from Columbia and had professed his love for her. However, the young girl rebuffed his advances because he wasn't a homeowner. In response, he wrote the girl back, insisting that he would soon have his mother's house as well as all of the money inside it.

A day prior to the murders, Moore headed to Columbia and checked into the Central Hotel under the pseudonym L. Smith. On December 17, 1912, he visited his mother's home, rusty axe in hand, and snuck in without her realising. As she was sitting in the living area, he crept up behind her and bludgeoned her to death. Then, the man headed upstairs to murder his elderly grandmother, beating her violently over her head until she lay bloodied and lifeless on her bed. Moore then fled the scene, dumping the blood-spattered axe in a ditch. He returned to the Central Hotel to clean himself up before checking out, but he forgot to clean the bloody bed sheets he left behind. The day after, he visited his mothers and alerted their neighbours to a most disturbing and horrific sight: his mother and grandmother had been murdered.

However, when the police arrived, they were immediately suspicious. They questioned Moore, discovering he'd stayed in the Central Hotel. They found the blood-stained sheets he'd left behind in his room upon further investigation. He was subsequently arrested and found guilty of double murder. The similarities to this and the slaying of the Moore clan were hard to ignore, but there was never enough proof to convict Henry Lee Moore of the massacre. Still, he remains a suspect.

Suspect #4: Paul Mueller

The 2017 book *The Man from the Train* suggests the Villisca Axe Murders were part of a much bigger crime spree by Paul Mueller, an immigrant who worked as a farmhand. He was the subject of an unsuccessful police search as the prime suspect in the 1897 murder of a family he worked for.

The book suggests that Mueller was guilty of the Villisca murders as well as a number of murders that took place over the span of ten years. They say his body count is at least 59 people and put forward their argument by offering a number of similarities to these crimes and the Villisca Axe Murder scene. In this case, the killer - Muller, would accost his victims when they were asleep, bludgeon them to death, and lock the property doors when fleeing the scene.

However, no solid connections were ever made despite the commonalities, and the culprit of the Villisca Axe Murders remained free to roam. The killer likely went to his grave without receiving punishment for his crimes. The case is still as cold now as back then, and the murder house remains vacant. Life carries on around the desolate property, although you can spend a night in the house if you're so inclined. There are tours of the house, and one of those packages offers you and a group of up to ten people with sleeping bags in tow to sleep over at the horror house.

The Teen Girl Bludgeoned to Death

Thirteen-year-old Billie-Jo Jenkins was beaten to death with a tent peg while painting the East Sussex family home in February 1997. Her foster father was the prime suspect and even spent six years behind bars for her murder before eventually being acquitted.

Billie-Jo Jenkins had a tumultuous early life, with her father being sent to jail and her mother unable to cope with being a single parent, the youngster was placed in foster care. From the age of nine, she was taken in by the Jenkins family, who by coincidence shared the same surname as their new family member. Billie-Jo was familiar with her newfound caregivers already, as she attended school with one of the Jenkins children prior to them taking her in. The family consisted of father Sion, his wife Lois, and their four young daughters. It seemed like Billie-Jo had finally landed on her feet after enduring an uncertain start in life, and her new family was highly thought of in the local area. Her foster father was deputy headmaster of the local boys' comprehensive school, they lived in an opulent area in the seaside town of Hastings, and Billie-Jo was popular with her schoolmates and teachers alike. By all accounts, she was studious, polite, and an all-around nice young girl.

On a cool Saturday afternoon, the last one before the half-term school holidays ended, Billie-Jo Jenkins carried out some household chores to collect extra pocket money. Lois had taken two of the Jenkins girls to the beach, and another was taking instrument lessons. With time to kill and extra money to be earned,

Billie-Jo set about ticking tasks off her list. Her foster sister was helping, too; she'd cleared out the storeroom but forgot to put back the tent pegs she'd removed from there while Billie-Jo was sweeping the outdoor patio, ready to paint the doors afterwards.

While the helpful teen was busy touching up the patio doors with a lick of fresh paint, Sion was busy picking up another daughter from her clarinet lesson. He brought his other daughter along for the ride, and when the family returned home, he decided to help with the painting. However, Sion remembered that they were out of white spirit and told his two young daughters that he'd need to head to *Do It All,* the local DIY place, to get some more. The trio drove towards the shop up the road, although Sion had forgotten to take any cash with him. The group had to return home empty-handed. When Sion headed through the house and stepped outside onto the patio, he discovered Billie-Jo on the floor, lying face first in a pool of her blood. She'd been brutally attacked and left to die.

It was reported that Billie-Jo's foster father had a tiny window of time to be the culprit. After picking up a daughter from her instrument lesson, he went into the house alone while his daughters waited outside in the car for him. It was worked out that he would have been alone with Billie-Jo for roughly three minutes or so before returning to his car and driving to the DIY store. However, it was suggested that those few moments could have offered Sion just the right amount of time needed to be maddened by something Billie-Jo had done - such as paint the patio door incorrectly - and beat her in a rage. He would then allegedly regain his self-control and return to his waiting children composed and calm before taking them on an unsuccessful trip to buy white spirit.

Upon returning home and making the horrifying discovery, Sion says he steered his young children into another room before crouching down next to a lifeless Billie-Jo. He says he inspected the badly wounded girl before calling an ambulance, also telling police that his dining room telephone - one of two in the home - was ringing, and he tried to quell the noise from the phone. It was put to the jury at his later murder trial that why, when his foster daughter was lying outside in a pool of her own blood, was Sion trying to stop the phone from ringing?

The prosecution had a number of rhetorical questions in their argument that Sion Jenkins was Billie-Jo's killer.

They suggested that Sion lied about his attempts to revive the lifeless teen and played both of the 999 calls he made to the court. In the first one, he was told by the operator to put Billie-Jo in the recovery position and also check for a pulse, things that the prosecution alleges he didn't ever try to do. They say this was proven when the paramedics arrived and discovered the girl still lying on her front, unmoved. It was then argued that when first responders asked the foster father if Billie-Jo was breathing, he replied that he 'couldn't say'. This doesn't correlate with what Sion would later say during police questioning, however. He told police that, when checking her injuries, she had bubbles coming from her nose, causing him to realise she was, in fact, still alive. It's alleged that he then shook his hands of the blood covering them before heading back into the house to wash them properly with soap and water. Sion said he was getting frantic by this point due to the ambulance still not showing up.

A neighbour who'd arrived at the house after being alerted to the commotion made a strange discovery. After examining a lifeless Billie-Jo, they spotted something sticking out of her nostril - it turned out to be a piece of bin liner. The neighbour pulled at the plastic emanating from the young girl's nose, causing a flurry of blood to rush out of her nostril.

Eventually, police cordoned off the Jenkins residence to carry out their investigation, including forensic analysis of the property and the crime scene. The family went to stay with neighbours as their home was scrutinised. A plethora of evidence was collected and used against Sion at his murder trial.

The Prosecution Flooded the Jury with Evidence

The prosecution team left no stone unturned and no detail left out in their case against Sion Jenkins. They argued that he'd flown into a fit of violent rage when he came home from picking his daughter up. It could have been that he was incensed by the lack of quality in her paintwork or because she'd turned up her music to an inappropriate level - no matter what the reason, it was suggested that Sion couldn't contain his hotheadedness. He spotted the tent pegs that had been left out, picked one up, and attacked Billie-Jo with a flurry of horrific blows.

There was also forensic evidence. The prosecution offered up the proof of Sion's bloodstained clothing. Tiny spots of blood, so small they could only be viewed microscopically, covered him from head to toe. His fleece, his trouser legs, and one of his shoes had microscopic dots of Billie-Jo's blood on them. The argument from the prosecution was that whoever killed the girl had to have been incredibly close to the teenager while they carried out their attack, and the tiny mist sprays of blood covering Sion were caused by him bludgeoning her.

On top of this, the prosecution made the jury aware that the father didn't even need to leave the house to buy white spirit as there was already half a bottle in the house. They argued that he did this to create a window of opportunity for someone else to have carried out the attack. They doubled down on this theory when they brought up the fact that he'd never taken any money with him when he went off to the DIY store.

There was also the strange route Sion had taken to the hardware shop. He didn't take the direct route, instead looping around the park twice before then heading in the right direction of the DIY place. It was alleged he did this to bide more time for himself, seeing as he didn't really intend to go into the store and buy the white spirit. It was also brought up about Sion's 'strange' behaviour after the murder, his lack of checking for a pulse, his lack of clarity in his 999 calls as to what happened to Billie-Jo, and his exaggeration of the time the teenager had been left alone. They also mentioned one particular act that struck them as odd behaviour: the foster father took off in the middle of Billie-Jo being seen to by the paramedics and began putting the top of his car up to protect it from the rain beating down. It was alleged he did this to offer up a logical reason as to why Billie-Jo's blood would have been found inside his car.

They also mentioned that the deputy headteacher had changed parts of his statement to be more in line with the statement his two daughters had given. For example, at first, he denied going back into the house before heading off to buy white spirit. He then changed his version of events, only when being made aware that his daughter's had told police he had, in fact, gone back into the house. It was noted how the dad had told police about 'prowlers' in the area, but the prosecution suggested this was a red herring since there were no police records about this. In a shocking move from the prosecuting team, they also suggested that Billie-Jo's foster father was having a sexual 'relationship' with the girl.

The Defence Team Rebuff the Prosecution's Allegations

The defence team offered a deflection for these accusations, insisting that if Sion had committed this murder, he'd be blatantly covered in blood. They agreed with the prosecution that the killer would indeed have been close to Billie-Jo, which is why Sion could not be the killer. If he'd bludgeoned her to her death, he'd have been splashed by her blood, much like the surrounding areas of the patio and trellis was.

They insisted that the tiny amounts of blood found on Sion's clothing were from comforting Billie-Jo when he first found her. As he crouched beside the young girl, he cradled her head, and the defence argued that as she took her dying breaths, this would have caused the microscopic spatters of blood on his clothing.

The prosecution team questioned why other people who came in contact with Billie-Jo around the same time didn't have the same tiny dots of blood covering them. The defence team countered that any third party didn't arrive on the scene for minutes after Sion had kneeled beside Billie-Jo, and by this point, she would likely have stopped breathing. There was also the murder weapon: the tent peg was only bloodstained at both ends, not where it had been held. Whoever attacked the girl would have large amounts of spatter over their hands and cuffs, but Sion didn't. Not only that, he wouldn't have had time to clean up or change his clothes in the short timeframe he was accused of being the killer.

The defence team put forward that Sion did not have enough time to be Billie-Jo's killer, particularly since he would have had next to no time to regain his composure after the rage-filled attack. There were no fingerprints on the murder weapon either. It was told how one of the paramedics who arrived at the scene noticed Billie-Jo had footprints on the back of her legs. However, the victim was quickly moved, and therefore the evidence was gone, but the defence noted how there was no dirt or mud on Sion's shoes to have caused the alleged footprints.

It was reported that there was another suspect in the murder; a man with known mental illness who'd been in the area around the same time Billie-Jo was killed. He was taken into police custody, and it was noted that he was behaving erratically at this time. In fact, police made an unusual discovery: the man had some plastic bag shoved up his nose, much like Billie-Jo. Still, police ruled him out as the killer since he was spotted in a location a quarter of an hour away from the Jenkins house when the murder happened.

The house next door to the Jenkins' was also desolate and boarded up, although it can't be ruled out that someone had broken in and was living there. Someone could have been sitting in wait, watching the family until they had the opportunity to strike.

Still, Sion was convicted of killing Billie-Jo and sentenced to life behind bars on July 2, 1998. He appealed immediately, but this was rejected. A subsequent case review of his trial saw his original conviction was quashed due to there being some evidence to suggest that Sion didn't commit the murder. When he was released, he accused the police of being incompetent. He was also physically attacked by some of Billie-Jo's relatives, who punched and kicked the dad of four as he left court. An aunt of the late teenager said that the judge at the trial hadn't allowed crucial evidence to be brought forward. Namely, she said that the bloodstains on Sion's clothes also carried tiny fragments of the girl's skull.

After he was acquitted, six years after initially being handed life in jail, Jenkins' ex-wife - who left him after his conviction - told the press how he was abusive, controlling and a compulsive liar throughout their marriage. She told how he would carry out physical punishments for indiscretions and that she and the children were at the mercy of his mood swings. She has since moved to Tasmania with her four girls, who have no contact with their father.

We will never know what really happened to Billie-Jo, but it's certain that her memory lives on for the people of Hastings. A local artist was so moved by the case that he made a memorial seat for the teenager, which remains in Alexandra Park. Her natural mother visits her grave weekly and places flowers down at Billie-Jo's resting place. She's also made calls to reopen the case to get justice for her child. Jeremy Paine, the now-retired detective who fronted the initial investigation into the horrific murder, thinks there is hope that justice will eventually be served. He thinks that advancement in forensic science coupled with the police's habit of periodically looking into historical cases with new technology will bring the spotlight onto the killer of Billie-Jo Jenkins.

The Keddie Cabin Massacre

The Keddie murders occurred overnight at Cabin 28 in Keddie, California, between April 11 and 12, 1981. Four lives were taken by an unknown assailant in a brutal fashion, and multiple suspects and cover-up theories have arisen in the decades since the bloody killings.

On the warm, sunny morning of April 12, 1981, 14-year-old Sheila Sharp was just heading back home after spending the night at the neighbours. Expecting to walk into her family just waking up, or even for breakfast to be cooking, Sheila opened the cabin door and was greeted with a traumatising sight: her mother, brother, and his school friend had all been viscously murdered. Blood stained the cabin floor and walls, and the three lifeless bodies lay on the floor. They were all still bound by the tape that had been wrapped around their wrists and feet to restrain them during the attack. The horrific scene that young Sheila walked into that morning became - and remains - one of the most seemingly senseless and macabre cold cases in America.

Laid in pools of their own blood were Glenna 'Sue' Sharp, her son John, and his friend from school, Dana. However, it became immediately apparent that there was someone else missing - Sue's daughter, Tina. Whether she was alive or dead was still uncertain, but it seemed like there may be a small chance the 12-year-old was still alive due to the killer(s) leaving three other survivors in the cabin. Sue's two youngest children, Rick and Greg, plus their friend Justin, were left unharmed in the bedroom next to where the massacre took place. Amazingly, none of the children heard any of the shrieking or commotion you'd expect from a bloody execution in the very next room. It was ascertained that the boys had slept right through the culling that had taken place just feet from where they lay.

Sue had moved into Cabin 28 in 1980, hoping for a fresh start after fleeing her abusive marriage and uprooting her children from Connecticut to the beautiful but largely uninhabited town in California. She had chosen this place in Northern California due to her brother living close by, offering her and her five kids some familiarity and security. An ironic thought considering just a year later, she'd be dead along with her son, his friend, and her daughter would be missing without a trace.

The evening prior to the attack on the family, young Sheila headed to her friend's house with little sister Tina, but the younger sibling headed back home to sleep. Sue's son John was with his friend Dana at a party in a town close by, but the pair returned home before the night had drawn to a close. Justin Smartt, a friend of Sue's two youngest boys, also stayed the night at Cabin 28.

Upon returning home the next day, Sheila would be met with a dizzying discovery, running as fast as she could back towards her friend's house to exasperatedly tell them her family had been massacred. Her friend's father raced up to Cabin 28 to confirm what Sheila saw really was true, but he was relieved to find not everyone had been a victim to the brutal attacker. He woke the three unharmed boys from their slumber and told them they needed to get dressed and come with him, lifting them out through the bedroom window, so they didn't have to see the bloodied and beaten corpses strewn throughout the cabin.

Blood Covered the Cabin Walls

There was no doubt the murders had been exceptionally savage. The killer or killers had certainly wanted to inflict pain and terror on their victims, and the vast amount of blood smeared all over the floors and walls indicated they'd done just that. The police were called to the bloodbath at Cabin 28, and once they arrived at the scene, they knew the caller wasn't exaggerating - the home was coated in crimson. It covered the victim's bedding, their bare feet, their bedside tables, the door frames, and blood had even been splattered onto the ceilings. Police noticed something unusual about the scene, too: the positioning of the blood suggested the victims had been moved around the cabin after they'd been murdered. They had been posed by the killer, but the answer as to why baffled the investigators.

John was the first corpse the police came across, and he had been left facing the ceiling with his limbs tightly bound by tape. His throat had been cut. His buddy Dana lay next to him with his head facing the floor. Dana's murder was particularly brutal: his face and head had been caved in by an object striking him multiple times. However, it seems this wasn't the cause of his death, as it would later be discovered that the killer had strangled the teen boy to death. Just like his friend, Dana had been bound by tape, and his legs were secured together tightly with electrical wire. This same wire was connected to John's legs, binding the two beaten corpses together.

Sue Sharp was the next victim to be uncovered. The mother of five had been crudely covered in a blanket, doing next to nothing to cover up the fatal attack she'd endured hours earlier. Sue's underwear had been taken off, she was naked below the waist, and the injuries covering her body showed signs of a struggle with her attacker. Just like her son and his friend, she'd been overpowered and restrained with tape. And, just like her son, she'd had her throat slit open. It seems the attacker had a gun with them since Sue had the imprint of the barrel of a pellet gun left on the side of her head.

Every victim had been beaten by various implements before succumbing to their fatal injuries. Each one had endured blows from hammers, a number of knives, and the claw end of a hammer. These items had been left, almost posed, on a table in the cabin.

The police were informed that there was one body missing - Tina Sharp. As soon as they realised they had a missing child on their hands, the FBI made their way to the crime scene. As they did, Sheriff Doug Thomas and deputy Don Stoy were being asked by locals what the motive for the massacre was. The officers were unable to find a motive, telling the local newspaper that the lack of obvious motive made the case a tough one to crack. It was noted that the cabin hadn't been broken into or showed any signs of forced entry. The culprit (or culprits) had taken the Sharp's phone off the hook and closed the curtains, making sure nobody would bear witness to the terror they were about to inflict. However, they did leave one of their fingerprints on the stair bannister.

More head-scratching than the lack of motive and any real evidence was the fact that the three boys sharing a room had all been left unscathed. As well as this, when questioned about what they may have heard or seen, each of the boys insisted that they knew nothing of the murders that occurred just feet away from them. While it's possible the boys had been in such a deep sleep that they heard nothing, particularly if the attacker was stealthy about their kills, it seems that wasn't the case. The Sharp's neighbours had reported hearing screams from the cabin next door between 1:00 - 2:00 am. They saw no signs of disturbance and couldn't quite figure out if the screams were actually coming from Cabin 28, so they headed back to sleep.

While the youngsters insisted they heard nothing during the attack in the early hours, the boys' friend, Justin Smartt, later told police that he saw Sue earlier that evening with two strange men. He described them in as much detail as he could remember - one had a moustache, the other did not - and told police that one of them was holding a hammer in their hand. He also confessed to investigators that he saw John and Dana return home from their party and fight with the strange men upon discovering them in the home. He recalled seeing one of the men take Tina outside through the back door of the home. This horrific crime was committed pre-DNA, so the only real evidence police had was the information Justin Smartt was offering them.

Subsequently, agents from the organised crime were sent in to help assist with the case. This was seen as strange at the time, seeing as there was no evidence pointing to the fact that the murders were a result of organised crime. Instead, it could have been seen as more beneficial to use the homicide unit, which was specially trained to piece together clues from crime scenes. Still, the Sacramento Department of Justice chose another unit to try and solve this complex case.

It wasn't long before two main suspects were under scrutiny from investigators. Justin's dad, Martin, was viewed as a possible culprit, along with his lodger, Bo Boudebe. The latter was a known criminal who was connected to organised crime. Witnesses had recalled that the pair had been dressed in suits the day of the Keddie Cabin murders and had been spotted at a local bar acting shiftily. While these things aren't incriminating as such, more pieces of suspicious information kept popping up. Martin, when interviewed by investigators, admitted that the hammer at the crime scene matched one he had. Oddly, he would continue, his hammer had disappeared just before the massacre. It would be months later before police discovered another weapon used in the murders: a knife, thrown in a bin outside of the local general store.

With no leads or tangible evidence, things got cold quickly. Years passed without a hint of a clue as to who committed the murders. However, three years after the crime, it seemed there might be a glimmer of hope in solving the case in the form of a macabre find.

Tina is Found

Butte County is roughly an hour and a half from Keddie, and in April of 1984, a man walking along Feather Falls stumbled upon a human skull. Close by was a plethora of potential clues: a child's blanket, a jacket, a pair of pants and a tape dispenser. Police were called, and they were sure the sad discovery was Tina Sharp. The murder tally for the Keddie Cabin murders was now looking like four, and a renewed interest in the case led to a strange phone call to the Butte County police department. The unknown caller told police that the remains they'd found recently were, in fact, Tina's, something only the killer could know. The child's remains were officially confirmed as Tina Sharp's two months later.

While this was going on, Sheriff Doug Thomas left his leadership of the investigation by taking a job at the Department of Justice in Sacramento. This left his handling of the case wide open for criticism, particularly from those closely affected by the crime. Sheila Sharp would later say that while acting as Sheriff, Doug Thomas told the two suspects that they should leave town instead of thoroughly investigating their possible role in the murders. It was also revealed that the call from the unknown tipster wasn't used as evidence and was left to collect dust amongst case files for almost thirty years. In 2016, a hammer believed to have been used in the attack was uncovered after the pond in Keddie dried up, exposing the rusted hammer in the mud.

Yet more information about the poor handling of the case was also coming to light after the case was yet again being looked into. It was revealed that Martin Smartt's wife had left her husband and fled their property the day the bodies were found in Cabin 28. Shortly after this, she went to the Sheriff's office with an interesting piece of evidence; a handwritten letter from her husband with what reads like a confession. In the letter, he tells his estranged wife that he bought her love by killing four people and expresses his disappointment at her choice to leave him after this. Unbelievably, this wasn't treated with any seriousness, and it wasn't looked into.

Sheriff Thomas rebuffed this by saying he'd already spoken to Martin and made him take a polygraph test, which he passed with flying colours. It wouldn't be until years later that it came to light that Martin and the Sheriff were close friends.

A counsellor who regularly spoke with Martin would later admit that the man confessed to parts of the Keddie Cabin massacre. The month after the murders, Martin headed to Reno Veteran's Administration, as he regularly did, but this time he confessed his dark secret to his counsellor. He admitted he killed Tina and Sue but denied being responsible for the death of the teenage boys. He says Tina had borne witness to the crimes, and seeing as she could easily identify him, had to murder her. The Department of Justice was made aware of this confession the same year the crime had taken place but didn't act upon the tip. In fact, they deemed it as hearsay.

There have been a few theories flung around as to what caused the attack on Cabin 28. One of the main ones is that it was a crime of passion following a love triangle involving Martin, his wife Marilyn, and Sue Sharp. Rumours suggest that Martin was sleeping with Sue behind his wife's back, while Sue was there for Marilyn as a shoulder to cry on about her abusive husband. It was said that Sue was trying to get Marilyn to leave her wayward spouse. However, it didn't take long for Martin to see what Sue was doing and enlisted the help of his lodger of ten days, Bo Boudebe, to help him carry out his murderous plans.

While just a theory, this version of events can help explain why Marilyn suddenly fled the marital home on the day of the murders. As well as this, it helps answer the question as to why the three young boys were left unharmed. Justin Smartt was asleep in the same room as Sue's two young sons, a fact that may explain why her boys were spared. This theory is also given some weight by the letter Martin wrote to Marilyn about taking the lives of four people to prove his love for her.

Both suspects are now deceased. Bo died in 1988, and Martin died of cancer in 2000. With advances in DNA, police have uncovered some forensic evidence that points the finger at other possible suspects. The new team looking into this case are confident the crime - and subsequent cover-up - involves more than just Martin and Bo. Interestingly, they've also said that they believe others involved in the destruction of evidence and Tina's death are still very much alive, which if true, is a chilling thought to comprehend.

Septic Tank Sam

The tale of a Canadian man who was discovered in a septic tank after being dumped there by his killer. His brutal death sent shockwaves throughout the country, and his true identity perplexed the police and public for decades.

Charlie and Mavis McLeod owned a farm in Alberta, Canada, in the tiny town of Tofield. On Wednesday, April 13, 1977, they headed to their mostly unused farm to pick up some items. The desolate smallholding they owned was home to various random items, so when the McLeods found themselves in need of a septic tank pump, they headed to their farm to hunt for one. What they'd find instead would haunt them forever.

Mavis headed to the septic tank and lifted the lid, only to be met with a sock floating in the water. She did a double-take only to discover a random shoe in the claggy water, and a closer look revealed that the shoe was attached to someone's leg. In a state of shock and panic, Mavis and Charlie raced to call the police, who rapidly made their way to the unpleasant discovery. Once they arrived, they began to empty the tank with the used ice cream tubs they had to hand. It was a tough task that took them over an hour to complete. The tank was two metres tall and full to the brim with water, in which the body had been left to decompose for at least a few months.

The man was fully dressed and had been wrapped up in a bedsheet that was bound with rope. You could tell from looking at the body that this was no tragic accident or suicide, but the subsequent autopsy would reveal the unknown man had endured unimaginable torture before his murder.

Now named 'Septic Tank Sam', the man had been cruelly burned with a blowtorch and had cigarettes put out on him. The killer had mutilated the man so badly that the medical examiner was unable to ascertain the gender of the body for months. It was concluded that the weapon used to mutilate his genitals was a sharp implement like shears. It was also speculated that the injuries he sustained could have been while tied up, possibly on a bed. The horrific torture the man suffered didn't kill him; it was multiple shots to his head and chest that ended the victim's hellish agony.

The killer, or killers, then covered the corpse in quicklime. This did nothing to accelerate the speed at which the body decomposed, but it's thought that the culprits had mistakenly thought it would. There was no way around the fact that the body had still decomposed over the months, which made identification near impossible. The pathologist estimated the man was under 40 years of age but likely older than 20 and was of Indigenous heritage. There was some hope that he could be identified, though. It took two exhumations for a 3D composite facial reconstruction to be created, showing the world what they thought the man had looked like. There were also sketches made up and distributed to news outlets in the hopes of someone recognising the man only known as Septic Sam.

As the years went by, the case remained cold. It seemed like there was little hope of ever finding out who the body was, let alone bringing the murderer to justice. All there was left for people to do was speculate and theorise. One of those theories was that Sam had been tortured so badly before his demise because he'd been exposed as a sexual predator toward young children. Of course, this was just local grumblings, possibly brought about as a way to explain how someone could harm another human being in such a sadistic fashion. The locals wanted to wrap their heads around this act, and the one thing they knew that would provoke such violence was if the victim was a child molester. There's never been evidence to suggest this was the case.

Sam's body remained in Edmonton Cemetery in an unmarked location for decades. Then, in 2021, something miraculous happened, something that rarely happens in cases like this.

Septic Sam's True Identity is Discovered 44 Years After His Body was Found

You may recall back in 2018 that the Golden State Killer was finally arrested after years of getting away with his terrifying murder spree. The events that led to his arrest are unique; he was identified after police sent the killer's DNA profile (obtained from a rape kit from one of his victims) to a well-known genomics site. The results eventually led to the arrest of Joseph James DeAngelo, a serial rapist and murderer who terrorised California in the 70s and 70s. Septic Sam's true identity was uncovered in this way too.

In January 2021, police submitted the still-unknown man's DNA for genealogy testing to see if they could finally give Sam his real name. In June of the same year, the police confirmed this to the public, announcing that Septic Sam was, in fact, Gordon Edwin Sanderson. He was 26-years-old at the time of his murder, and he was indeed Indigenous, as the examiner had suspected decades earlier. With this breakthrough, the police contacted his surviving family and informed them of the sad news. Despite the upsetting news, the eventual identification could still go some way in offering closure for the victim's relatives.

By all accounts, Gordon, or Gordie as his loved ones called him, had endured a tough upbringing. He had been taken away from his family in 1959 as part of the 'Sixties Scoop' - which saw Indigenous children in Canada being taken (or 'scooped') from their parents and placed in foster homes. By the time he was in his 20s, Gordon had moved to Edmonton, settling there. He had family in Calgary, who he was due to visit prior to his murder. He never made his prearranged meeting with his brother, and his sudden disappearance was never reported to the police, causing his true identity to remain unknown for over four decades.

It's thought that Gordon was killed by people he associated with in his criminal exploits. His identification allowed police to access his records, which showed Godon to have had several dealings with the police, as well as someone who struggled with substance abuse. His killer is presumed to be someone who also resided in Edmonton, but they may be no longer alive.

Still, as this case shows, the unexpected can happen, and forensic science is making breakthroughs at a rapid pace, so I wouldn't rule out this case being solved at some point in the future.

Texarkana Moonlight Murders

A mysterious murderer named 'The Phantom Killer' stalked the city of Texarkana in the 40s, prowling the night to mercilessly slay young couples in their cars.

The border from Texas to Arkansas lies an amalgamation of both states: Texarkana. The city is home to 37,000 inhabitants and boasts a rich history and numerous sightseeing spots. However, the thing it's most famous for is something Texarkana would rather forget. The city is well-known for its Federal Courthouse, which takes pride of place on the state line between Texarkana, Arkansas and Texarkana, Texas.

In late February 1946, 19-year-old Mary Jeanne Larey was cosying up to her boyfriend, 25-year-old Jimmy Hollis, in his car. The young couple had parked up on the quietest road they could find to get some alone time. They'd just been to the movies, but the couple weren't quite ready to head home just yet, so they headed on a detour down lover's lane. It wasn't quite midnight when the couple was interrupted by a man shining his torch through the car window.

The couple was startled not only by the fact they'd been interrupted at such a late hour but also by how the man was dressed. More specifically, he had a cloth mask covering his face, almost like he'd taken a pillowcase and cut eye and breathing holes in it. Sure it was a prank, but still unimpressed by the abrupt interruption, Jimmy told the man that he'd bothered the wrong people. Hoping the strange man in the mask would take the hint, the young couple remained in the car. 'I don't want to kill you,' threatened the man, 'so do what I say.' The panicked couple got out of the car, prompted by the pistol in the unknown man's hand.

The man demanded Jimmy take his pants off. Despite Jimmy's compliance, the attacker suddenly struck his victim in the head with the pistol. As his victim lay on the ground, the aggressor continued to whip Jimmy with the gun. Mary was frozen with fear as her boyfriend was being attacked, and she was sure he'd been shot. She heard loud bangs that resembled gunshots, but in reality, those deafening sounds were Jimmy's skull being bashed in. After his violent attack on her boyfriend, the masked man turned his attention to Mary.

He stormed over to her, grasped the muzzle of his gun, and whacked her across the head with the butt of the pistol. His violent acts were followed by orders for Mary to run away, which she did, although aware her tormenter may just be toying with her. Despite the high heels making the getaway slower than she'd like, Mary raced towards the nearby road that was sure to bring a passing car. With safety within eyeshot, Mary felt a blunt object striking the back of the head, and she fell to the ground. The masked maniac loomed over the vulnerable girl before kneeling down beside her and using his gun to sexually assault Mary. Devastated by the attack and crippled with fear, Mary told the man to just kill her.

By sheer luck, an oncoming car and its shining headlights startled the masked attacker, and he fled the scene, leaving Mary beaten and traumatised - but alive. The teenager was able to run to a nearby house where the police were called. Mary and Jimmy were raced to the hospital to have their injuries seen to. While the attack was brutal, it wasn't fatal for the couple, and the pair went on to make a full recovery, physically at least. But one thing stalled police in their search for their attacker: Mary and Jimmy's descriptions of the masked man were wildly conflicting. Mary believed the man was African American, while Jimmy said the attacker was white. Both recalled the man as being about 6 feet tall, but that seemed to be the only correlating piece of information they told police. This made law enforcement suspicious of the pair; they thought the couple knew the hooded man was and were lying to throw police off the scent.

With no leads or an accurate description of the attacker, the police could do little. However, the unknown assailant wouldn't lay low for long. The following month, on March 22, he reappeared and turned the violence up a notch.

Polly Ann Moore, 17, and her older boyfriend, Richard Griffin, 29, were sitting in Richard's car on a remote road often used as a lover's lane by young couples. Motorists didn't frequently pass where the pair were parked, but one eagle-eyed passerby caught a glimpse inside of the car. He thought the couple in the car was sleeping, but he uncovered the horrific truth upon closer inspection. Richard was slouched in the front, his head being propped up by his hands, and what may have looked like an uncomfortable sleeping position to the passerby soon transpired to be a murder scene when he saw bullet holes in the side of the man's head. A glance in the back of the car revealed another gruesome discovery: Polly was laid face down across the back seats. The police were quickly summoned to the macabre scene, and they just as quickly realised they had a dangerous person on the loose targeting young couples. They found just one piece of evidence: a .32 cartridge shell. They released little information publicly about the double-murder, but local rumours swirled throughout the city suggesting Polly had been raped. Locals were stunned by the spate of attacks in the area and began taking extra security precautions just in case. Still, they didn't expect yet another brutal attack just weeks later.

On April 14, young Betty Jo Booker had just finished her set playing the saxophone at the Veterans of Foreign Wars club. The 15-year-old was a promising student who adored performing just as much as she did obtaining straight As. When her set was done, she met up with Paul Martin, her 17-year-old friend whom she'd grown up with. He planned to drive the girl home, but the pair decided to stop off at Spring Lake Park before calling it a night. The park was mere minutes from Betty's home, which makes the events that followed all the more frustrating.

Martin's body was discovered first. He'd been shot in his shoulder, through his hand (suggesting self-defence), his face, and one shot went through the back of his neck right through the front of his skull. It seemed that with each attack, the killer was becoming increasingly violent. After the tragic discovery of Martin, the search was on for Betty, whose body was nowhere in sight. There was a glimmer of hope that the teenager would be found alive, and a search party was quickly rallied to find Betty. The search team spread out, and just before midday, they made a discovery. They had found the young girl, but it wasn't good news. She'd been shot in the torso and the face and was laying on her back underneath a tree. Yet again, the victims had been killed with a .32 pistol.

Despite being fully clothed when found, it was revealed that Betty had been raped. Her clothes had been put back on, and her body was staged afterwards. Her hand was placed in her pocket while her coat had been fully buttoned up to her chin. Further ballistic testing on the .32 shells found at the scene was discovered to be from the same gun the same as the prior double murder. This was now a hunt for a serial killer.

The community was overcome with fear. One of them was a crazed killer, and nobody had a clue who it was. A curfew was introduced, and sundown was a cue to return home. Local businesses even closed their doors early to ensure they and their customers could get home before the masked attacker roamed the streets at night, even the gun shops that were seeing record sales as fear gripped Texarkana. The townsfolk even pitched in to raise money to offer as a reward for the killer's arrest. They knew the masked man would still be prowling come sundown, and they would do what they could to protect their families. They didn't need to wait too long before *The Phantom Killer* - as the press now dubbed him - struck again.

Virgil Starks settled into his armchair on a warm evening of May 3, turned on the radio, and pulled out the daily paper. It was the 37-year-olds nightly relaxing ritual, and he would often be joined by his wife, Katie. This evening had panned out like most others: the pair had supper, cleaned up, and planned on relaxing in the living area before they headed to bed. For reasons still unknown, this night would end being senselessly violent and would cost Virgil his life.

As Katie tended to chores upstairs, she heard glass shattering from downstairs. She raced to the living area to find her husband standing in the middle of the room, with a frightful look on his face. Blood rushed down the side of his face, dripping down onto his torso. He stumbled as he looked at his wife, eventually collapsing in his chair where he succumbed to his injuries: two gunshots to the back of the head.

She raced over to help her husband, but the devastating realisation that he was dead forced Katie to confront the fact that there was a killer in the house - and he was coming for her next. She ran to the phone and barely managed to pick it up when the killer reappeared from the same window he shot Virgil and pumped two bullets into Katie's face at close range. By some miracle, the woman survived the attack.

Not only that, she even managed to get up after being shot, despite believing the killer was very likely now inside the home. She couldn't know this for sure due to the steam of blood filling her eyes, but she did manage to pick up the couple's pistol and run as fast as she could to a neighbour's home. Despite being horribly wounded, Katie was now safe and would recover from the horrific attack. She was rushed to have surgery, and police attended the operating room to get a statement from the distraught woman.

The Phantom Killer had stuck again. Texarkana braced itself for another attack.

A month passed without anything. Then another. And another. Slowly but surely, the locals let their guards down, and they scrapped their curfews. Bizarrely, the Phantom Slayer didn't strike ever again. The abrupt way he started and ended his killing spree only makes this case more intriguing. The suspect list was long, and the rumours about who the killer was were rife. Hundreds of people were arrested in the hunt for the masked madman, and the police even had a number of false confessions to the murders. Out of the hundreds of suspects, three men stand out as being of particular interest.

Suspect #1: Youell Swinney

Seasoned criminal Youell Swinney was a well-known car thief. He was initially arrested for stealing a car, but the lead investigator in the Moonlight Murders had some circumstantial evidence that put Youell on his radar as being The Phantom Killer. The night Polly Ann Moore and Richard Griffin were murdered, a car from the area had been stolen while another stolen car was left abandoned. This could have put Youell in the area if only based on loose evidence. However, the suspicion toward the car thief would only escalate.

Police waited for the thief to come back and collect his abandoned car, believing they'd catch Swinney red-handed, only to find his wife Peggy was the one who arrived to reclaim it. Peggy was swiftly arrested and almost immediately told police her husband was the masked killer roaming the streets at night. Her confession went into some detail, too, and she explained how her husband murdered young couples and even told police where he hid the victim's possessions. Although police were somewhat dubious about her confession - it wasn't always consistent from interview to interview - they thought it might be her way of avoiding incriminating herself in the murders. When investigators went to verify the truth of her statement, they did find that she was being honest: all the victim's items were located where she said they'd be.

With the abundance of circumstantial evidence against Youell stacked up with Peggy's admission, police had a heavy case against the criminal. Peggy's revelations proved to be the most important part of their case against Youell, particularly that she'd been able to divulge information only the killer would know. However, she ended up retracting her statement. Without this, police had a weak case against their suspect.

Because of this, Youell was never charged with the Moonlight Murders, but he was jailed for his persistent car thefts in 1947, not long after the killings abruptly ended. He was released in 1978.

Suspect #2: Henry Booker Tennison

Teenager Henry Booker 'Doodie' Tennison was still a freshman when he killed himself in November 1948. The 18-year-old penned a note before his suicide in which he confessed to being The Phantom Killer. He would have been just 16 when he carried out the murders if he was telling the truth.

Police looked into the confession but found little to tie the young man to the crimes. He did attend the same school as Betty Jo Booker, but that was as far as any connection he had to the slayings went. The pair weren't friends, perhaps acquaintances at best due to their involvement in the school band. As well as this, Henry (often referred to by his nickname 'Doodie') had an alibi for the night Virgil Starks was killed. According to Henry's friend, the pair were playing cards together when news broke of the attack at the Starks' property.

Why the teenager would confess to such horrific crimes if he wasn't responsible is anyone's guess. There could be several reasons why: coercion, mental health battles, or perhaps there was something even more sinister at play.

Suspect #3: Ralph B. Baumann

Former machine-gunner in the Army Air Force, Ralph Baumann, handed himself in to police and claimed to have spent weeks unaware of where he was or what he'd been doing. His sudden awakening from his fugue state happened the same day Virgil Starks was killed, and Ralph also realised his rifle was gone. In a state of panic, he hitchhiked from Texarkana to LA, unsure if he was responsible for the killings, but ended up going to Los Angeles police after becoming 'his own suspect'. However, it soon transpired that Ralph was diagnosed as 'psychoneurotic' by the Army Air Force and was released from his position there because of this. On top of this, he'd previously admitted to murders he'd not committed, so police disregarded his confession, and he was free to go.

As the years went by, many more men were arrested and questioned. More even admitted to the crimes, but their confessions were quickly quashed or rebuffed. Any leads were always met with a dead end, and the Texarkana Moonlight Murders are unlikely to be solved.

Still, the legend of the masked killer lives on, and the story has been made into two films, both called *The Town That Dreaded Sundown*. The 1976 version of the film is often shown in Spring Lake Park, Texarkana, around Halloween, ensuring the locals don't forget The Phantom Killer and his reign of terror.

The Sheppard Murder Case

The controversial case of Dr Sam Sheppard, a neurosurgeon suspected of killing his wife, who insisted it was a wild-haired being who slaughtered his spouse.

In the small hours of July 4, 1954, Marilyn Reese Sheppard suffered a brutal and fatal attack in the home she shared with her husband, Samuel Sheppard. Before Marilyn's death, the Sheppards had been entertaining guests at their luxury lakeside property before Sam fell asleep while lounging on their daybed. Taking this as a cue to end the dinner, drinks, and movie night, Marilyn escorted their guests out of the Bay View home and headed upstairs to bed. Just hours later, she would be dead.

Sam was jolted from his slumber by his wife's cries for help in the early hours and raced up the stairs to their bedroom, only to be met with what he would later describe as a 'white form' attacking his wife. This 'tall, bushy haired' being then set his sights on Sam, who beat the doctor unconscious. When Sam finally came around, he raced to his son's bedroom to make sure he was still there. Luckily, the 7-year-old was fast asleep, seemingly unaware of the horrors that had been going on around him.

Sam then raced down the stairs to apprehend the intruder, but after catching up with him by the lakeside, he was once again beaten unconscious by the attacker. Once he came to for a second time, he raced back to his house, somehow losing his t-shirt and his watch on the way. By now, it was around 5:30 am, and the only thing a panicked Sam could think to do was to call his friend, mayor Spencer Houk. The mayor and his wife raced to the Sheppard's house after hearing Sam cry down the phone, 'I think they've killed her.'

This would be the same story Sam would tell the Houks and the police. When Spencer and his wife entered Sam's home, they found him sitting in a swivel chair, clutching some injuries to his neck. After listening to his version of events, Bay Village police were called and arrived at Sheppard's residence at around 6:00 am.

When law enforcement arrived, they headed upstairs to the crime scene. They were met with a horrifying sight. Marilyn was lying on the marital bed, face-up, covered in her own blood. Her top half was exposed, and her pyjama bottoms had been pulled down. Her face didn't look human anymore: it had been beaten so violently that she was deemed unrecognisable. More than twenty blows with a blunt object had rained down on Marilyn's face, leaving her pillowcase crimson and her blood spotting the walls around her. It wasn't just the 30-year-old woman who was tragically killed that night - it was her 4-month-old foetus, too. Marilyn would have had a baby boy if her life hadn't been heinously taken away.

By this point, Sam's brother had turned up at the scene, and the police were under the impression that this was a botched robbery. After all, valuable items had been taken, and the house of the affluent couple was in a state of disarray. There was nothing to suggest the Dr had anything to do with the crime since he too had been badly beaten by the attacker. However, County coroner Sam Gerber arrived on the scene and didn't think things were as clear cut as police initially suspected. In fact, he thought the crime scene looked staged.

With the coroner inspecting the house, Sam was transported to the hospital to seek treatment for his head injuries. Coroner Gerber noted there was no forced entry and no clear murder weapon. In fact, he pointed out that the trail of blood from the murder scene down the straits leading outside looked like the blood dripping from the object used to kill Marilyn.

Gerber followed the trail of blood, looking outside for any clues or evidence. Sure enough, in a nearby bush, he found a bag with Dr Sheppard's missing watch, plus a key and a ring. The coroner believed that his discovery proved the robbery was faked in order to provide an alibi for the real killer - Sam Sheppard. He figured Marilyn had been murdered around three that morning. Her watch had stopped at 3:15.

With his suspicions high, he wanted to speak to the only witness to the murder and the person he suspected of committing the brutal crime. Gerber quickly made his way to the hospital, where Sam was being treated with the intention of getting to the bottom of his undeniably wild story. There was no denying the notion of a strange creature randomly attacking the Sheppards sounded farfetched at best, but Gerber was also taken aback by Sam's seeming lack of emotion in his police statement.

Subsequently, Sam Sheppard refused any more probing from Gerber or the police. He was sticking to his story and insisted he loved his wife, but he would no longer answer any more questions. After all, his doctor had ordered his patient to decline more questioning. However, his doctor was also his brother, Stephen. Sam also refused a lie detector test, further fuelling the rumours of his guilt.

The more investigators delved into Dr Sheppard's life, the more they felt like he was Marilyn's killer. As the days went on, police uncovered a number of things that could offer up possible motives for Sam to kill his wife.

The Sheppard's neighbour told investigators that Sam wasn't able to have any more children due to his continuous work with x-ray equipment, rendering him infertile. With Marilyn four months pregnant at the time of her death, this would point to an extramarital affair on her part, thus causing Sam to retaliate to this news with violence. The foetus was autopsied, but his paternity wasn't ever disclosed.

Allegations of extramarital affairs plagued the Sheppards - on Sam's part, mostly. Police didn't need to dig too deep to find out Sam had been seeing a nurse from the very hospital he worked in was now being taken care of at: Bay View Hospital. Police kept this information to themselves until Sam agreed to go to the station for voluntary questioning. Here, they asked him outright about his relationship with nurse Sue Hayes, and he immediately denied ever being anything but close friends with the woman. Police knew he was lying - Susan Hayes confirmed as much. His denial of the affair further led investigators to assume his guilt.

A fortnight after the violent killing, the Cleveland Press published a front-page story requesting a public inquest. Coroner Gerber heeded the newspaper's demand and acted upon it. He subpoenaed Sam to an inquest, to which the press and the locals took a keen interest. So much so that it's since been branded a 'media circus'. Coroner Gerber was the judge and jury while the crowd jeered and yelled. The inquest lasted three nights, where Sam was probed about his marriage and sexual affairs. His attorney was made to sit at a distance from his client, although at one point, he was provoked enough by the heckling from the audience that he stood up and challenged the crowd's jeers. He was quickly ejected from the inquest by Coroner Gerber.

It was at this hearing that Sam publicly denied any affair with Susan Hayes. This lie would come back and bite him further down the line. In the meantime, the Cleveland Press was still making headlines calling out for Sam to admit his guilt. Feeling the pressure from the press and the Bay View residents, Gerber had Sam arrested and promptly charged with the murder of his wife. Just over three months after the killing took place, Sam Sheppard stood trial accused of coldly taking his wife's life and that of his unborn son.

Day one of the trial began with a press tour of the crime scene. Sam Sheppard was handcuffed and chaperoned around the property for all to see. Then the trial resumed at the courthouse, where the jury was shown explicit photos of Marilyn and her injuries. Despite Sam asking to be out of the room while these shocking photos were circulated, his request was denied. He was made to look.

Coroner Gerber took the stand and offered up his incriminating evidence. He told the jury how Marilyn suffered injuries from a surgical tool - one only Dr Sam Sheppard would have the knowledge to use. The fact that no such weapon was ever found wasn't questioned, nor was the fact that Sam's attorney was blocked from much of the supposed evidence against the doctor. As such, Sam's defence was unable to argue against Coroner Gerber's accusations. Perhaps the most damning witness was yet to take the stand - Susan Hayes. When she took the stand, she admitted she had been seeing the doctor behind his wife's back. All eyes were on Sam, who cracked under the scrutiny and admitted she was telling the truth. The odds seemed stacked against Sam, whose integrity and innocence were quickly evaporating away before the eyes of the jury.

Still, his defence had some promising evidence to put forward. Three witnesses had come forward to say they'd spotted the 'figure' Sheppard had described to police. The witnesses told the court how they saw the wild-haired being around the Sheppard's property in the early hours of the morning while driving past the property. The doctor's seemingly far-fetched story surprisingly had witnesses, something nobody expected.

Still, Sam Sheppard was found guilty after less than a week of jury deliberation. He was spared the guilt of first-degree murder since there was no evidence to suggest Sam had planned the attack. He was handed life behind bars for second-degree murder.

Sheppard Maintained His Innocence

Tragically, just weeks after his sentencing, Sam's mother killed herself. Adding to the heartache, his father died of natural causes a week later. Apart from being allowed to attend his parent's funerals, Sam was detained in his maximum security jail for almost a decade. All the while, he was fighting the sentence handed to him. His brothers, still believing their sibling was innocent, did all they could think of to get Sam's ruling overturned. One of the avenues they ventured down was to hire a new forensic scientist to analyse the crime scene. When viewing the images of the bloody scene, Dr Paul Leeland Kirk noticed that the blood spatter hit all the walls - except for one part. The area devoid of any blood would likely be the place where the killer stood, thus meaning the murderer would have been covered in Marilyn's blood. When the mayor and the police attended the Sheppard property, Sam was noticeably clean aside from one pool of blood on his trouser knee. Should he have been the killer, he would have been covered head to toe in blood, Dr Kirk said.

As well as this, from analysing the blood spatter, Dr Kirk could tell the murder weapon - whatever it may have been - was brandished by a left-handed attacker. Sam Sheppard wasn't left-handed. The evidence suggesting Sam had been falsely imprisoned didn't end there. The forensic scientist also revealed that Marilyn's teeth found at the scene had been from biting her attacker with so much force her teeth had broken. Sam had no bite injuries on his body whatsoever. With all of this promising newfound evidence collated, it would seem a retrial would be on the cards. However, this wasn't to be - the judge rejected the new findings.

The only thing Sheppard could think to do was the one thing he'd declined to do for years - a polygraph test. In his pursuit of a reliable polygraph expert to carry this out, Sheppard came across a man named F. Lee Bailey who specialised in lie detectors. Bailey immediately became heavily involved with Sheppard's bid for freedom and believed he never received a fair trial. As he trudged through all the evidence, he found a crucial piece of evidence. The newspaper reporter who wrote daily about the Sheppard case noted how the judge at the first trial told her prior to the trial taking place that Sam Sheppard was guilty and the trial was only going ahead as a 'formality'. Subsequently, Sheppard's sentence was ruled the result of a mistrial, and he was released on November 16, 1966.

Sheppard's medical licence was handed back to him, and he got married to a woman he'd been writing to while in prison. Despite spending a decade in jail, it seemed like Sam was going to start life afresh and had landed back on his feet. At 40-years-old, he had his whole life ahead of him. However, the promise of a better future didn't last. Sam hadn't had his medical licence back for very long before multiple patients died while being operated on, causing lawsuits to be filed against him for malpractice. It was rumoured he carried out surgeries while drunk, and his reliance on alcohol was well known. After this, his wife left him, causing Sheppard to further turn to the bottle.

In a bizarre new career venture, Sam then became a professional wrestler. His in-ring name was 'Killer' Sam Sheppard, and his reputation brought in fans by the droves. He married the daughter of his wrestling coach six months before his death in April 1970. His excessive alcohol use caused his liver to fail at the age of 46.

The story doesn't end there, however.

Sam's son, Sam Jr, affectionately named Chip, set out to clear his father's name. In 1997, Chip began a civil suit against Cuyahoga County on behalf of his late father for his 1954 imprisonment that he deemed wrongful. Subsequently, the bodies of Marilyn and Sam were exhumed for further analysis. A civil trial presented a new suspect: a man named Richard Eberling, who used to clean the windows on the Sheppard's Bay View property. In fact, Eberling, a known criminal, was arrested in 1959 for theft. When detectives trawled through his ill-gotten gains, they found rings that had belonged to Marilyn Sheppard. Eberling insisted he took the rings from Sam's brother's property, which he'd burglarised the year prior. When probed further about the murder, Eberling told police his blood was at the murder scene but insisted it was because he cut himself while cleaning the window panes and protested his innocence. Still, the story didn't quite add up, and a polygraph test was carried out.

Eberling, a man known for violent tantrums, compulsive masturbation and a limited ability to acquire language, passed the lie detector. He was asked a range of questions about Marilyn Sheppard and his involvement in her murder, and it was deemed he was telling the truth when he denied any involvement. However, years later, the results would be reevaluated by expert polygraphers who mostly concluded the test showed Eberling was being deceptive. The ones that didn't agree that the results showed he was lying said the test was inconclusive. As the years passed by since the murder, new DNA technology had been introduced - the types of testing that weren't available in the 1950s. New analysis found blood from a third person at the crime scene.

A forensic analyst was able to conclude that they were almost certain one of the blood spots tied the crime back to Richard Eberling. However, almost certainly doesn't hold up in court. Eberling was never convicted of the murder of Marilyn Sheppard, but he was handed life behind bars for the murder of Ethel May Durkin, an elderly woman whom Eberling was employed to take care of. While caring for the older woman, he confessed to the murder of Marilyn to his co-worker, Kathy Dyal. It was also reported he confessed his guilt to another inmate while in prison.

Eberling passed away in 1998, taking the truth with him to the grave.

The Boy in the Box

The heartbreaking story of a young boy whose beaten body was discovered discarded in a cardboard box. While his identity is unknown and no one was charged with his murder, there have been some believable theories as to what happened to the malnourished little boy.

One headstone at the Ivy Hill Cemetery in Cedarbrook, Philadelphia, differs from the rest. It has no name etched on the gravestone. Instead, it reads 'America's Unknown Child,' a tragic yet accurate description of the young boy who's buried underneath it. Frequently adorned with teddies and toys left by the strangers who still think of the abused boy, the grave is a sobering reminder of the chilling crime that remains unsolved.

In winter 1957, a hunter was trawling through the woods in Fox Chase, a neighbourhood in Philadelphia. He'd set muskrat traps earlier and was returning to the woodland to check them, and while hacking his way through the brush, he stumbled upon an ominous-looking cardboard box. The hunter cautiously opened the box and peered in, shocked at the horrifying sight. The box wasn't big, but it still managed to hold the decomposing body of a young boy. The young hunter made a choice not to notify police about the boy in the box and instead carried on checking his muskrat traps. He didn't want to tip the authorities off about his illegal hunting, so he left the box as he found it and resumed his day.

Despite the box being left in a relatively remote area, it would only take a couple of days before someone else came across the boy in the box. A student was driving past the woodland when he spotted a rabbit making its way from the road into the bush filled with traps. The young man got out of the car and followed the rabbit, later telling police he did so to make sure the bunny didn't get snared in one of the traps he knew covered the woodland. While rummaging through the thicket, he found the small box, opening it to discover the body of a bruised and beaten young child inside. He considered the idea that telling the police about his discovery would incriminate him and thought about the consequences of leaving the boy in his cardboard coffin. However, he quickly overcame his fear of going to the police and decided to report the disturbing find.

The Investigation Into the 'Philadelphia Box Boy'

There was no doubt about it - the boy in the box was very young, but upon taking a closer look at the corpse, it wasn't easy to ascertain his age. He was so small and malnourished that he could have been three years old, but his face looked a bit older, more like a seven-year-old. The horrifying state of the youngster made it hard to believe the boy was properly cared for by his family. He was dirty, emaciated, and covered in injuries up and down his tiny body. His hair had been crudely cut, with clumps sticking up in random places. The police were given the difficult task of trying to track down the boy's parents, but it became clear that his mother and father weren't searching for the child, making it a difficult task for authorities.

They did fingerprint the boy in a bid to ID him, but his prints weren't on file. After all, this type of information is often only obtained by police from a criminal, not from children, but there weren't many other leads for police to follow. All over Philadelphia, flyers were stuck on shop windows, fences, and anywhere people may happen to be passing. Hundreds of thousands of these flyers were printed and sent to local businesses, hoping that someone - anyone - would be able to help identify the young boy. Despite the extensive reach of the missing posters - some were even folded into gas bill letters before being sent to homeowners - nobody claimed any knowledge about who the child was or what happened to him.

The outcry of shock and sadness that the crime provoked slowly died down as the case went cold. However, as time went on, theories as to who the unknown child was and who caused his death swirled. There are two main hypotheses about the child, the first one originating in 1960, three years after the little boy was found.

Hypothesis #1 About The Boy in the Box

A man named Remington Bristow worked at the medical examiner's office that dealt with the unknown child's remains. The case affected him so much that he spent a great deal of his time looking into it, even outside of work, going as far as getting in touch with a psychic in order to get closer to identifying the boy. The psychic was brought to the location the child was found and subsequently guided a hopeful Remington to the local foster home. Prior to attending the crime scene, the psychic had described a building similar to the foster home, telling investigators to look for such a place in order to find out who was responsible for the death of the boy in the box. It seemed like there may be a speck of light at the end of the tunnel for Remington, who desperately wanted to solve the case.

The police didn't have any evidence linking the foster home to the boy, let alone a reason to obtain a warrant to search the premises. Luckily, however, the owners were holding an estate sale, and the police attended to see if they could find anything tying the home to the child. They did find a few things of interest: hung on the washing line were blankets the same as the one the child was wrapped in inside the box. They also picked up on another potential clue: a baby's cradle inside the home. While not exactly incriminating, it does provide some (albeit circumstantial) connection to the home: the boy's box, his makeshift coffin, was for a baby's cradle from JCPenney, much like the one set up in the foster home.

After the visit, Remington theorised that the little boy's mother was the stepdaughter of the foster home's owner. He believed the boy's mother and her stepdad worked together to keep the child's existence quiet, and when he died, they disposed of him in the woods. Remington thought that the pair didn't want to expose the child's mother as having children out of wedlock but thought the boy's death was likely accidental.

There was no real evidence to charge the foster family with the crime, so this avenue was eventually abandoned until 1998 when the investigation again turned its attention to the owners of the home. Police in Philadelphia joined up with a group called the Vidocq Society, a team of retired policemen who collated in 1990 to help with unsolved murders in the Philly area. With the help of the Society, police interviewed the owner of the foster home and his stepdaughter. By this point, they were no longer dad and daughter - they were husband and wife. Despite this raising suspicions even further, police closed this line of inquiry indefinitely after interrogating them. There was nothing but circumstantial evidence and Remington Bristow's hunch they were responsible to tie them to the little boy in the box. The case remained silent until 2002 when another theory was explored.

Hypothesis #2 About The Boy in the Box

Over 40 years after the boy's body was found, a woman who was only named 'M' or 'Martha' approached the police with a disturbing story. She said she knew the boy and gave the police his name. She claimed that her mother, who she accused of being abusive, bought the little boy and put him through years of sexual molestation and physical abuse.

It took over three hours for M to detail the child's short but torturous life. She began in 1955, making her 11 when her story started. She told how her mother, a respected librarian, drove her to a big house, presumably a children's home from the description she gave, and headed into the home clutching an envelope. When she emerged, she brought a young boy out with her. M said that in hindsight, the envelope contained money, and she believed the boy, who was named Jonathan, was purchased by her mother. The child lived with M and her mother in Philadelphia, but family life was far from bliss.

M explained that Jonathan didn't have a proper bedroom, much less a proper bed. He was banished to the basement, his bed made from bits of unwanted cardboard. If he needed to use the bathroom, he was to use the basement drain. Disturbingly, M told how her mother abused Jonathan and how before she bought the boy, her mother would sexually molest her. Now that Jonathan was there, she turned her attention to the new child, regularly abusing the boy physically, sexually, and emotionally. M said that the sole reason she believed her mother bought the youngster was purely to abuse him.

His untimely death came about when M's mother became incensed when Jonathan was sick while she was bathing him. The cruel mother hit the boy's head on the floor numerous times for this, resulting in his death. She then cut his hair in an effort to stop police from identifying him, loaded his little body into the car and took M with her to dump him in the woods near Fox Chase.

The story is plausible because M told authorities that Jonathan vomited up his last meal of baked beans. There had indeed been baked beans in the boy's stomach when he'd been autopsied. The detail about him being bathed just before his death also matched up with coroner findings that the child had wrinkly fingers like he'd been submerged in water. These details had never been made public, and only the police knew what was on the coroner's report.

There was also another factor helping corroborate M's sad story. As the mother and daughter were disposing of the little boy's body, a helpful man driving along the same road pulled up and asked the pair if they needed help, completely unaware of what they were disposing of. M says she was ordered to make sure the man wasn't able to note the licence plate while her mother gratefully declined his offer of help. The man got back in his car and drove off but didn't forget his encounter with the strange mother and daughter. He went to the police after The Boy in the Box was found, further validating M's version of events.

There was just one problem with her story. Or, rather, with M herself. The police were reluctant to believe her because she'd had a history of mental health issues. The mere mention of mental health problems in a witness, even in 2002, meant authorities were disinclined to put much stock into her accusations. M's childhood neighbours also dismissed her claims completely. Despite the fact that the woman was able to offer up facts only the police would know - such as the boy had long hair that had been cut short - it was believed she fabricated the tale. She had told her psychiatrist this tale thirteen years prior to going to the police, but due to client confidentiality, it never went further than the inside of the psychiatrist's office. The investigators dealing with M pointed out, however, that no notes of this 1989 confession to her psychiatrist exist, so this couldn't be put forward as evidence her story was true.

This theory eventually fizzled out, and nothing was ever officially corroborated with M and her statement to the police.

While this case is undoubtedly tragic, there is a small comfort in the fact that the little boy is still thought of by the people of Philadelphia, although it's heartbreaking to note that he's been shown more love and compassion in death than he did throughout his short life.

Who Was Mr Kipper?

Suzy Lamplugh was a British woman reported missing in July 1986 in London. She was due to meet a person she referred to as 'Mr Kipper' before her disappearance.

July 28, 1986, was a normal day for Suzy Lamplugh. She was at her job as an estate agent, and her workday was filled with showing clients their potential new properties. Normally after showing a house, she would return to the office and check in with the other office girls. On this day, though, she headed out of the *Sturgis and Sons* office just after lunchtime to meet a client but never came back. That summer's day would be the last time anybody saw Suzy alive.

As she made her way to meet the client, Suzy carried only her bare essentials: her car keys, her house keys, a little cash and credit cards, but left her handbag back at the office. After all, she wouldn't need it while showing a prospective buyer around 37 Shorrolds Road. The potential purchaser was 'Mr Kipper' - or, that's what Suzy called him in her work diary. She was to meet him at the property at 1 pm, and she did, in fact, meet a man at the location at that time. The pair were seen together, walking away from Shorrolds Road.

Suzy's coworkers were getting worried about her as the day passed, and there was no sign of her or any sort of communication from her. It wasn't like her just to take off and not come back to the office, particularly since she'd left her handbag at her desk. Just before 7 pm, a manager at Sturgis and Sons called the police to report her missing.

Suzy's mother was informed her daughter hadn't returned from a viewing, and the police double-checked the 25-year-old hadn't dropped by to see her parents throughout the day. She hadn't stopped by. Her mother, panicked and worried, waited for the police to update her, hopefully with the news that Suzy had been found alive and well. They didn't find Suzy, but they did find her company car. It had been left not too far from her work office, and although the vehicle was unlocked, there were no signs of anything untoward. In fact, her purse was still in the glove compartment. The car keys were gone, however. Her mother, upon hearing the news, headed straight to the abandoned car with Suzy's father. They even brought their dogs with them to see if the canines could get a scent of their daughter and lead them to her. The search, however, was fruitless. Police ended up sending the heartbroken pair home as, in their own words, they were 'getting in the way' of police investigations. Diana and Paul Lamplugh did as the police asked and faced an anxious and sleepless night ahead as they waited for any updates.

The next day, Scotland Yard announced Suzy's possible kidnapping to the nation amid their increasing concerns for her wellbeing. Aside from this broadcast, there was no movement on Suzy or what may have happened to her. The following day, on July 30, Diana turned 50. By this point, her London house was swarming with journalists, cameras, and some concerned public. Eager to try anything to help find her daughter, she allowed the press to enter her home, and the next day, the Lamplugh's were on both of the main breakfast TV shows in the UK. Both *GMTV* and *Breakfast Time* aired interviews with the parents, during which Diana spoke of how she thought Suzy was still alive but being held against her will. She added that her daughter was fit and strong, so she remained hopeful that she would be able to fight her way out of danger.

The press coverage was gaining traction, and strangers were finding ways to contact the Lamplugh's directly. They sent letters, cards, and even some personal anecdotes of Suzy to them via post. The case had struck a nerve with not only the locals but also the nation. It hit home that this could happen to anyone: Suzy was thought to have been taken against her will in broad daylight, a concept that showed crimes like this weren't so far-fetched. They were reality.

As time went by, Diana's tone shifted from hopeful to admitting that Suzy could be dead. While she acknowledged her daughter had likely been killed, she understandably couldn't bear to broach the subject of the parts between her abduction and her eventual murder. Her father also commented that Suzy was claustrophobic, and the idea that she'd been kept locked up somewhere would have been terrifying for her. The parents agreed that the idea of her being dead was easier to deal with than the thought that she was locked up somewhere suffering at the hands of her abductor.

Years passed with no movement on the case. As Diana told the press, it was as though she'd been erased by a rubber - there was no trace of Suzy, of any tangible evidence - nothing. Despite her body never being found, Suzy was legally declared dead in 1993.

The Prime Suspect

Convicted murderer John Cannan was, and remains, the only suspect in the abduction and murder of Suzy Lamplugh. A number of things tie him to the crime, some indirectly, but the M.O of Suzy's sudden disappearance matches that of Cannan's prior predatory endeavours.

He had abducted 29-year-old Shirley Bank while she was out shopping, and it's thought he kept her at his home for some time before beating her to death in 1987. He then dumped her body in the woods. He was handed three life sentences for this brutal murder, as well as the attempted kidnap of another woman and the rape of a woman in 1986.

Authorities interviewed John Cannan over Suzy's disappearance for a number of years. He was brought in for questioning in 1988, 1989 and 1990. A decade passed when police had nothing more to probe John about, but a re-investigation in the 2000s saw him brought back to answer police questions.

There are several reasons why he's the prime - and only - suspect in the abduction and murder. Firstly, John looks like the man Suzy was last seen walking away from Shorrolds Road with. The photo reconstruction of the man Suzy met was an uncanny resemblance to the man they nicknamed 'Kipper' in prison. This is another clue - or coincidence: the man Suzy was due to meet called himself Mr Kipper. It's been said John Canaan's strange nickname came from his preference for wearing kipper ties.

Other circumstantial information came to light when John was arrested for the murder of Shirley Banks. When police searched his property, they found he'd repainted Shirley's car and attached a fake number plate to it. It read SLP 368. Police were led to think this was a macabre nod to Suzy's murder. *SLP* stood for Suzy Lamplugh, while the 386 contained the year of her kidnapping, 1986. It was also hypothesised the plate could have been a hidden clue, such as coordinates to the location where Suzy was buried. Using the fake plate number as coordinates would give a location close to the army barracks in Worcestershire. Coincidentally, this is where John had told a former girlfriend he'd buried Suzy. However, this couldn't be used as evidence since the woman later retracted her statement.

There was also an interview John himself had with detectives that could have been viewed as odd. When probed about the number plate, the suspect admitted that the choice of letters and numbers could have been seen as incriminating, but he insisted he picked the number plate lettering randomly. He also made outlandish claims about where he obtained the car, going as far as saying he bought it off a killer car dealer who was the person responsible for the deaths of not just Shirley but also Suzy. He also said this 'Bristol businessman' who sold him the car had killed another girl. It was common knowledge that John Cannan was a car salesman himself and did business in the Bristol area. It sounded like John was simply describing himself. Detectives probed him on this, asking if the businessman was him, to which John agreed it was. That was the breakthrough police needed - until John quickly retracted his admission and refused to continue with further questions.

Years went by, and the case seemed ice cold. However, the investigation was reopened in 2000, where more implicative evidence was found. Most of this evidence was either left uncovered during the initial investigation or had been deemed inconsequential at the time.

Firstly, John had been released from a stint behind bars just days before Suzy went missing. He was in an open prison, meaning he could have had plenty of opportunities to meet with or watch Suzy before her kidnapping. At the same time, she was complaining to a family member about a man she was seeing. The unnamed man was apparently from Bristol - where John's family lived - and he was beginning to scare Suzy with his behaviour.

Another seemingly incidental comment from John aroused suspicion. He claimed to police he'd never been to the Fulham area - where Suzy was last seen - despite that being where he was in an open prison. More than this, he was also frequenting the area when he was out on day release.

Several witnesses had come to police to tell them they'd seen a man resembling John sitting in a BMW on the day of Suzy's disappearance. In the passenger seat was a woman who looked like Suzy, and the pair were spotted arguing. What looked like a lovers tiff ensured the witnesses didn't intervene, but the sighting also bore other interesting coincidences. The BMW John was allegedly sitting in was a left-hand drive and painted dark - exactly like one he'd used to commit other crimes in. These cars were uncommon, rousing suspicion towards Cannan even further.

The circumstantial - yet nothing ever concrete - evidence continued to pour in.

In the days before Suzy vanished, John turned up at a house with a *For Sale* sign outside, seemingly thinking the young woman inside was alone. He made the woman feel uneasy with his odd behaviour, but her partner soon turned up, and John hastily left. He was also spotted at the Sturgis and Sons office building where Suzy worked, peering into the windows. He was pressed by police about his strange movements around the time Suzy went missing, and John couldn't provide an answer; in fact, he couldn't remember his whereabouts for the first three days after he was released from jail. He did, however, have clear details of all the other days he spent out of jail.

While there was an abundance of information placing John Cannan in the same area as Suzy around the time of her vanishing, it was eventually found that there wasn't enough tangible evidence to convict him of her disappearance or murder. In a telling display, the police were open about their certainty that John Cannan was responsible for Suzy's tragic end but admitted they had insufficient evidence to bring him to justice.

While he sat behind bars, John made a number of remarks that alluded to his guilt. One of the more disturbing ones was to his psychiatrist. He claimed he was thinking of divulging everything about the fate of Suzy, but would only do so when his mother died. It could be unlikely he ever does, and he's eligible to apply for parole in 2022.

In the wake of their daughter's disappearance, Diana and Paul Lamplugh created *The Suzy Lamplugh Trust*. It helps counsel the family members of missing people, as well as educate people about the dangers of stalking. They offer advice on how to intervene should you see a bystander being harassed, an act that could very well have altered Suzy Lamplugh's fate altogether.

The Lamplugh's were awarded the title OBE in the years before their deaths. Paul died in 2018, while Diana passed away after her battle with cancer in 2019.

The Lake Bodom Massacre

In the summer of 1960, an unknown assailant brutally attacked four teenagers as they camped in Finland. Three of the teens tragically died, but one survived. The killer still hasn't been caught.

Espoo is a small but picturesque city not too far from Finland's capital, Helsinki. Close-by there is the equally beautiful Lake Bodom, a peaceful area covered in pine trees that hosts an abundance of nature and calming greenery. The shoreside is serene, the surrounding forest is filled with tranquil sounds, and the villages nearby could be pulled straight from the front of a postcard. Despite all of its serene beauty, Lake Bodom is remembered for something entirely more sinister: the 1960 triple murder that took place upon its shore.

On a warm June weekend, two couples pitched up their tents along the tree-covered Lake Bodom shore, hoping to soak up the peaceful surroundings. The friendship group was made up of 15-year-old girls Irmeli Björklund and Tuulikki Mäki and their 18-year-old boyfriends, Seppo Boisman and Nils Gustafsson. After enjoying a day at the lakeside, they retired to their respective tents around 10 pm. Three of the teenagers wouldn't make it to see the next day.

The murder scene was that of a slasher film. Blood covered the tents, with two of the victims still laid inside, while Nils Gustafsson and Irmeli Björklund were found outside of their tent, laid on top of it. The killer had brutally attacked each of the teens, using a knife from the outside of the tents and using the sharp blade multiple times to mutilate each of the victims. As well as a knife, there was evidence the killer also had another weapon, an unknown item that was used to cause blunt force trauma to the group. The vulnerable group had little chance against the attacker, all of whom were asleep when he snuck up to their site and brutalised them.

The attacker singled one person out specifically when doling out their depraved acts of violence. Irmeli Björklund's clothes had been removed from the waist down, and her body was covered in knife wounds. Some of these wounds were inflicted upon her after her death, suggesting the killer was fueled by rage and not just a lust to kill.

The attacker, after murdering the trio of teens, scoured the campsite and took a number of items. The knife used in the crime was never found, nor was the secondary weapon, which has been suggested could have been a rock picked up from the shoreside. Among the random items taken by the criminal were motorcycle keys belonging to the male teens, although the bikes themselves weren't stolen. The odd things that were moved from the scene included Nils Gustafsson's shoes, which were abandoned about half a mile from the campsite.

The group was estimated to be attacked in the very early hours, sometime between 4 am and 6 am. Around 11 am, the horrific scene was discovered by a passerby, who immediately called the police. When they arrived, they were greeted with a disturbing sight; three of the teenagers were pronounced dead. Nils Gustafsson, however, was found injured but alive beside his mutilated girlfriend. It was noted that Nils had significantly fewer wounds than the rest of the group - he endured a broken jaw but was spared the brutality of the knife, unlike his girlfriend and friends. He was taken to hospital before the area was searched by police, who allowed civilians to walk through the site, contaminating potential evidence or removing it altogether. Investigators then requested the aid of soldiers to help them find the items taken from the tents, further contaminating the crime scene.

There Was No Shortage of Suspects

Nils Gustafsson's recollection of events was sparse in details since he claimed he'd been the first person the killer attacked. Therefore, he was unconscious throughout the slaughter but did mention he saw the perpetrator just before he was knocked out, claiming the attacker wore an all-black outfit and had bright red eyes. Police didn't follow up on Nils as a suspect right away, but there were a plethora of other people who found themselves on the authorities' radar - in fact, they even had a confession to the murders. Pentti Soininen was a renowned criminal with equally as famed violent tendencies, and he apparently told a fellow inmate he was the Lake Bodom attacker while he was locked up with him in the 60s.

There was some circumstantial and far-fetched evidence to support the idea that he could have been the attacker. He lived close to the lake at the time the murders took place. However, the police never took much stock in his claims since he would have been just 14 when the teens were murdered. In 1969, Pentti hung himself. It was June 6 - the same date the Lake Bodom killings took place nine years earlier. Still, it's unlikely Pentti actually committed the crimes, but because he placed the blame on himself and seemed to take such an interest in the case, it was worth mentioning his part in this tragic story.

Aside from this, there were other notable suspects:

Suspect #1: Karl Valdemar Gyllstrom

For years, Karl Valdemar Gyllstrom was seen as suspect number one by police. He told a friend of his that he killed the teens at Lake Bodom. He did this while heavily drunk and quickly denied his confession ever happening upon sobering up. Aside from this, there's little concrete evidence to tie Karl to the crimes but there's a heap of circumstantial evidence and suspicious coincidences. He was known locally as having a hatred for the people who camped along the lakeside and was feared among the local community. Police were hesitant to follow up on his alleged confession as he was seen as being 'deranged' by the locals, someone to be avoided due to his antisocial behaviour.

His actions would often teeter from antisocial to downright violent, especially for those who visited Lake Bodom as tourists. He would regularly cut down the tents of those camping beside the lake and would even throw rocks at strangers who dared visit his town. It was later discovered that Karl was seen walking home from Lake Bodom the morning the killings had taken place, but due to his aggressive tendencies, nobody felt comfortable enough to inform the police about this potentially vital piece of information.

Then, just days after the brutal lakeside murders, Karl was witnessed behaving unusually in his back garden. He had a well in his yard, which he was filling with concrete. It was hypothesised that he could have been getting rid of the undiscovered murder weapons.

Yet another piece of evidence suggested Karl was responsible for the killings, and this time, it came directly from his wife. Initially, she'd provided an alibi for her husband when the teens were attacked but would later go back on her assertion that she'd been with Karl on that fateful June morning. Instead, she told police that her husband had threatened her life if she incriminated him, causing her to lie about him being fast asleep when the murders took place. This means his whereabouts is unknown at the time of the killings.

Karl Gyllstrom drowned himself in 1969, killing himself in the deep waters of Lake Bodom, closing this line of enquiry altogether. While there was an abundance of incriminating facts to implicate Karl, there was never any hard evidence found to prove he was the murderer.

Suspect #2: Hans Assmann

One of the most notable suspects in the Lake Bodom massacre was Hans Assmann, who walked into Helsinki Hospital in bloodstained clothing and muddied hands on the morning of June 6, 1960. He was unkempt, incoherent and behaving very oddly. In fact, he faked unconsciousness in order to be seen more quickly by the doctors. His behaviour wasn't tolerated for long, however, and he was made to leave the premises before being seen.

It was after this altercation with hospital staff that Hans went home and shaved off his striking, long mop of blonde hair. This random act of hair cutting tied in with some children coming forward to police to tell them about the 'blonde man' they saw at Lake Bodom at roughly the same time the killings took place. It was also interesting that the description the children gave police matched Hans, even down to the clothing he was wearing when he visited the hospital that morning.

There was no denying that his behaviour was suspicious, particularly when coupled with the children's statement to the police. Again, however, there was no tangible evidence to tie him to the killings, just a lot of heavy suspicion. It can't have helped that Hans had been a suspect in a number of other murders prior to the Lake Bodom massacre, including the murder of Auli Kyllikki Saari. The 17-year-old's murder is one of Finland's most notorious unsolved murders, and the case only ever yielded three suspects, one of the primary ones being Hans.

Suspect #3: Nils Gustafsson

The only survivor of the massacre, Nils managed to find normality in his life after the attack, getting married and having children. Four decades passed without a genuine suspect being uncovered, and it seemed like the horrific murders had all been forgotten about by the authorities. However, forensic evidence had come a long way since the '60s, and Finnish police had enough new evidence to reopen the case in 2004.

The breakthrough evidence, according to prosecutors, suggested that Nils was heavily intoxicated on the morning of the murders and had been thrown out of the tent by his friends. After this, Nils retorted by attacking Seppo Boisman, resulting in one of Nils' injuries: a broken jaw. It was alleged that the drunk and enraged teen then killed his friends. This version of events was presented at the 2005 trial, in which Nils stood accused of being the perpetrator of the Lake Bodom massacre.

His defence lawyer refuted that story and insisted Nils was in no state to kill three people, given that he'd suffered injuries himself, including some stab wounds.

The prosecution countered this with the new DNA evidence found on Nils' shoes, found half a mile from the campsite. It was ascertained by police investigating the crime in 1956 that the killer had worn Nils' shoes at some point throughout the attack. All of the victim's blood had been discovered on his shoes, but his own blood was notably absent. This was an important piece of information for the prosecution team, who used it to argue that Nils' blood wasn't on the shoes because his injuries didn't happen at the same time as the others. They said that after brutally stabbing his girlfriend and friends to death, he hid the shoes in an attempt to make the scene look like an intruder had stolen them after they'd attacked the group.

Then, he took the same knife used to slaughter the other teens and stabbed himself before laying next to his girlfriend's corpse, feigning unconsciousness, waiting for the scene to be discovered. The prosecution also noted how Nils' girlfriend, Irmeli Björklund, suffered the most violence at the hands of the attacker, suggesting her killer had a personal vendetta against the young girl.

In October of 2005, Nils Gustafsson was acquitted of the Lake Bodom killings. There wasn't enough conclusive evidence to convict him, nor could they find a strong enough motive for the then-18-year-old to have carried out such savage murders. Plus, the crime scene hadn't been thoroughly closed off at the time, resulting in a number of questions concerning the reliability of evidence found. Nils was subsequently paid out a large sum of money for the time he spent on remand, although a request to sue the Finnish papers for their coverage of his trial was declined.

Adding to the mystery of the Lake Bodom killings comes from a sketch of the potential killer, created after police hypnotised Nils in order to get him to mentally retrace his steps on that June morning. They thought hypnosis might dig out some buried memories, and they did manage to get enough details from Nils to create a composite sketch of the attacker he described.

At one of the victims' funerals, a photograph was taken, and upon getting it developed, it was discovered a man bearing an uncanny resemblance to Nils' description attended the funeral. Nobody knew who this man was. Picture quality in the '60s wasn't anywhere close to the quality we have nowadays, but it was irrefutable: the man in the photo looked just like the sketch. It was thought the unknown funeral attendee was Hans Assmann, but this wasn't ever corroborated.

It's been over six decades since the bloody massacre, it's fair to think that the killer, or killers, won't ever be brought to justice. While the perpetrator may very well be dead or now old and harbouring their murderous secret, the Lake Bodom massacre certainly hasn't been forgotten about in Finland. For years after the crime, children were told to beware of the mysterious killer, and the unknown boogeyman was a cautionary tale told to make children more aware of being safe when they're at the lake.

The Strange Case of Teresita Basa

Teresita Basa was found brutally murdered in her Chicago apartment in 1977. Police eventually arrested her killer, an event some people believe wouldn't have happened if her ghost hadn't tipped police off about her murderer's identity.

True crime and supernatural stories sometimes cross paths.

Think of the Elsa Lam case, the tourist found dead in a cistern on the roof of the infamous LA hotel, *Stay on Main* (formerly named *Hotel Cecil*, a place famous for a huge number of deaths and suicides happening there). After she was found, CCTV was checked to retrace her steps and see who could have killed her. What was discovered on the film was perplexing - Elsa was acting erratic, scared even. The video captured her strange movements and gestures, particularly when inside an elevator. The doors mysteriously remain open despite Elsa pressing every button to close them. It looked like she was talking to someone who wasn't there or visible on camera. These were her last moments, caught on camera before she disappeared. She was subsequently found engulfed in water in the hotel's cistern.

This case drew considerable interest worldwide, and the intriguing footage of her last moments caught on camera went viral. No one was ever arrested for her murder, and there have been several conspiracies and theories floating about as to what really happened to Elsa, some of which broach the supernatural. There's been plenty of speculation that her death was other-worldly, particularly online and in true crime forums.

The case of Teresita Basa also offers a paranormal element to it, with the ghost of the deceased allegedly tipping the police off about the person who brutally killed her. While, unlike other cases in this book, this crime has been solved, there's no denying the events that led to the arrest of the culprit are mysterious.

The Killer Tries to Hide A Brutal Murder

Teresita Basa moved from the Philippines to Chicago, seeking a better quality of life. Here, she found work as a respiratory therapist at Edgewater Hospital and was known by her coworkers as shy but incredibly reliable. She lived a quiet life with her husband, Joe, and her passion for music saw her offer the neighbourhood kids free piano lessons. Her introverted personality and kind nature meant the eventual murder of the 47-year-old all the more shocking when her corpse was found.

On February 21, 1977, the apartment block where Teresita lived was evacuated after the strong smell of smoke filled the building. Her neighbours had told the janitor about the ominous smell, who subsequently called the fire department. Once all of the tenants were outside of the building, firefighters discovered just where the smoky scent was coming from: Teresita's apartment. The door was kicked down, and the firemen did their job, putting the blaze out quickly. However, it was evident that the fire didn't start on its own, and it was clear it wasn't accidental. In fact, the apartment had been set on fire to try and hide a more macabre crime: a murder.

The police were called, and the investigation uncovered more unpleasant details. Teresita had been stripped of all her clothing, and as she lay lifeless on the floor, a big butcher's knife protruded from her chest. Her clothing had been strewn over and around her to help get the fire going, as well as her mattress, which had also been set alight. It was clear the killer had tried to incinerate every bit of evidence that tied them to the senseless murder of Teresita.

It was initially assumed that the woman had been raped since she had been found naked. It transpired, to everyone's surprise, that she hadn't been violated in this way after the autopsy concluded that no sexual assault took place. Sexual assault as a motivation for murder was suddenly taken away as an avenue to go down for the police, who were already struggling to find clues and leads. Add to the fact that the fire had burned through a lot of the apartment, thus any possible evidence, and detectives felt like they were at a dead end. Miraculously, among the charred remains of her belongings, police found a note written by Teresita, which offered one possible clue. The note said, *Get theatre tickets for A.S.* With no other leads, officers set out to find who A.S could be.

Interviews took place over the following month. Her coworkers, old school friends, her neighbours in the apartment building, and anyone who'd been in contact with the woman recently were spoken to. Again, police found themselves hitting a brick wall. There was no apparent motive, the unassuming woman had no enemies, and she'd not reached out to loved ones or police about any concerns about her safety. The case was set up to turn cold incredibly soon. But, six months later, something miraculous happened.

Teresita Talks From Beyond the Grave

Remibias 'Remy' Chua, a coworker of Teresita's from the hospital, approached the police with a strange story. The woman went to detectives after having recurring dreams about her old colleague. In these unsettling dreams, Remy told how Teresita would plead with her to report her killer to the police. Remy's husband corroborated his wife's story, too; he told detectives that while in the middle of one of these dreams, his wife began talking - but the voice didn't belong to Remy. The unfamiliar voice claimed she was called Teresita Basa and confided in Remy's shocked husband that she was murdered. She also gave him the name of her killer: Allan Showery.

While Remy's husband had no idea who Allan Showery was, Remy, did - he worked at the hospital too.

When she was told about her strange sleep talking, Remy had no recollection of it. Plus, her husband was reluctant to go to the police with this information - who would believe them after all? They would be going to the authorities to tell them the ghost of Teresita had visited them and told them who killed her. Because it sounded so unbelievable, they feared going to the police would put them at the top of the suspect list. The pair were going to forget about it. But, there was one person who wasn't going to forget: Teresita.

Yet again, she returned to Remy as she slept and spoke aloud to her husband. She asked him why he hadn't gone to the police as she asked. The husband was honest and said he didn't have any solid evidence - that the police would dismiss him and think he was crazy. Then, Teresita - channelling through a sleeping Remy -

dropped a bombshell piece of information. She said Allan Showery had taken some of her jewellery after killing her and that his girlfriend was wearing it. This nugget of information was enough to prompt Remy to take her unusual tale to the police.

As you can imagine, authorities were hesitant to investigate these claims, but since there were no other leads, they decided to look closer into Showery. He could, after all, be the A.S initials Teresita had written about on the piece of paper.

Investigators were taken aback to find that once they delved deeper into Showery, he proved to be quite a good candidate to be the prime suspect in the murder of Teresita Basa. He lived close to her, and after a bit of digging, they found he was due to drop by Teresita's apartment on the night of her murder to fix some of her appliances. Once they had this tidbit of information, they pulled Showery in for questioning, and he did admit to visiting her that night but insisted he left early as he didn't have the tools required to fix her TV properly. Unconvinced by his retelling of his movements that night, the police got in touch with Showery's girlfriend. This would be the break they needed to capture the killer.

The girlfriend told police Showery had recently gifted her some jewellery and handed it over to authorities for examination. Teresita's loved ones were shown the items and confirmed they'd belonged to her. Showery was immediately arrested and presented with the damning evidence, which saw him confess to the murder. He said that he had initially left her home but intended to return and steal any items of value. However, he was unaware that Teresita didn't own much of value, nor did she keep much in the way of cash with her. In the end, he settled for her jewellery, which he gifted to his girlfriend.

When confronted with the fact that Teresita was found naked, the killer admitted that he wanted to make it look like a sexual attack on the woman before she was murdered. Still, that wasn't the case closed: he decided to plead not guilty at the trial, which eventually ended in a hung jury. Showery was sent back to jail as a retrial was being arranged, during which he had a sudden change of heart; he decided to plead guilty. It was rumoured that the reason for his drastic choice of plea was because Teresita - or rather, her ghost - had visited him while he sat in prison. However, it could have been that a guilty plea would offer Showery a reduced prison sentence rather than an admission of remorse.

The tale of Teresita Basa understandably made the news for the unusual yet effective way the case was solved. The fact the case was seemingly solved by the person who was murdered from beyond the grave was an intriguing notion. As for Remy, she still insists that her strange dreams and sleep talking were the result of her being possessed by Teresita. Detectives involved in the case also don't entirely dismiss the idea the case was solved by the supernatural; in fact, many support it as there is no other explanation as to how Remy knew the information she did.

Although, there are some who believe the other explanation, one that wasn't as widely accepted.

Although Remy was insistent that the deceased woman's ghost is what prompted her to go to the police, it turned out that Remy and Showery weren't just coworkers, they had a strong dislike for one another. In fact, Showery was the reason Remy lost her job at the hospital after complaining about her to their bosses. Still, if this were the case, and Remy went to the police out of spite, how did she know about Showery taking Teresita's items and giving them to his girlfriend?

Ultimately, regardless of what caused Remy to go to the police, her doing so ensured the case of Teresita Basa didn't go cold, and her killer was brought to justice.

****

Thank you for reading *Mysterious Murders: True Crime Tales of Unsolved Murder Cases and Mysterious Deaths*. I understand this book has more questions and open endings than it does answers, which can often be a source of frustration for true crime enthusiasts. However, I truly believe that these crimes can't be forgotten, because time and time again it's been proven that even the coldest of cold cases can still be solved. Even if it's too late for the killer(s) to be brought to justice, at least the victim and their family can have the last act of closure of knowing who carried out an unthinkable crime.

I'm currently writing Volume 2 of *Mysterious Murders*, where I'll cover crimes that have intrigued me for years, such as the Dardeen family massacre, as well as cases new to me such as the tale of the so-called Shark Arm Murders, which is as perplexing as it sounds.

If you liked this book, discovered an intriguing case you'd not heard of, or are fascinated by the dark nature human beings are prone to exhibit, please do follow me on social media. Likewise, if you have any ideas for future books you'd like to see me write, any feedback you'd like to offer me, or perhaps a true crime story of your own, then find me at DrewCrimes.com or search Drew Creeden on all platforms.

I look forward to hearing from you!

Drew.

www.ingramcontent.com/pod-product-compliance
Lightning Source LLC
Chambersburg PA
CBHW061324120726

48001CB00002B/679